JEWELRY FROM NATURE

JEWELRY
FROM
NATURE

45
GREAT
PROJECTS
USING
STICKS & STONES
SEEDS & BONES
■

CATHY YOW

LARK BOOKS
Asheville, North Carolina

Editor: Jane LaFerla
Art Director: Kathleen Holmes
Photographer: Evan Bracken
Production Assistant: Hannes Charen

Library of Congress Cataloging-in-Publication Data
Yow, Cathy
    Jewelry from nature : 45 great projects using sticks and stones,
    seeds and bones / Cathy Yow.
        p.   cm.
    Includes index.
    ISBN 1-57990-107-7
    1. Jewelry making.   2. Nature craft.   I. Title.
  TT212.Y69   1999
  745.594'2—dc21   98-48217
                                                   CIP

10 9 8 7 6 5 4 3 2 1

First Edition

Published by Lark Books
50 College St.
Asheville, NC 28801, US

© 1998, Cathy Yow

Distributed by Random House, Inc.,in the United States, Canada,
the United Kingdom, Europe,and Asia
Distributed in Australia by Capricorn Link (Australia) Pty Ltd.,
P.O. Box 6651, Baulkham Hills Business Centre, NSW 2153, Australia
Distributed in New Zealand by Tandem Press Ltd., 2 Rugby Rd.,
Birkenhead, Auckland, New Zealand

Printed in China by Donnelley Bright Sun Printing Company, Ltd.

ISBN 1-57990-107-7

DEDICATION

To the staff and volunteers of the Nature Discovery Center Friends of Bellaire Parks Bellaire, Texas

CONTENTS

Jewels for the Taking

I began making jewelry from natural materials several Christmases ago after reading a journal article about botanical jewelry. Since my creativity championed my funds for gifts that year, I was inspired to make a few beads out of whatever seeds I could find in my own neighborhood and fashion them together as presents. I was surprised to find that a simple seed or twig or pebble could become an attractive jewelry component.

Gallery: *Shell Brooch by Cathy Yow*

While this book is primarily about transforming objects from nature into personal adornments, it's also about going outdoors, looking around, and learning about the natural world around you. The most intriguing aspect of this pastime is that extraordinarily lovely raw materials are a part of everyone's environment, whether in town or country. My own neighborhood is a low, swampy spot in the heart of a modern city. Yet, in the small area I cover by car, bicycle, or on foot, I've harvested the majority of the materials used in making the jewelry in this book.

You needn't travel to distant habitats to find the unusual and exotic. Only a few strides from my front door are plants whose true homes are far afield: camphor trees from China and Japan, palm trees from world tropics, the gingko of ancient time and lore, mescal bean trees from West Texas and New Mexico, and jasmine from India. You'll find that each new material you discover, whether it comes from near or far, will offer you the opportunity to learn something about its origins and uses.

Gallery: *Corn Jewelry by George Corona*

History, Fable, & Lore

Making jewelry from natural materials is an elegant metamorphosis that complements both the object and its wearer. Seeds, twigs, bones, pebbles, seashells, and even human teeth have been used for human adornment in almost all cultures at some time in their history. Spices were strung into necklaces in Asia, bone beads were made and worn by Native Americans, and coconuts have provided food, clothing, and ornament to many cultures.

Beads and Natural Jewelry From Around the World
Clockwise from upper left: *olive wood beads from Israel; Bedouin clove necklace; beetle wing necklace from the rain forest; snake vertebrae necklace from Africa; green sea shells; rudraksha beads from India; candlenuts from Hawaii*

Gallery: *Seed Leis from Hawaii* Left: *Canna indica, Spohora chrysophylla, Mucuna urens, Vigna marina, Delonix regia*
Middle: *Canna indica, Canavalia kauaiensis, Mucuna gigantea, Caesalpinia pulcherrima, and puka shells* Right: *Canna indica, Erythrina sandwicensis, Bauhinia monandra*

Many of the materials found in this book have been used since the beginnings of civilization because they are rare, beautiful, medicinal, or have religious significance. Countless materials are available today that have wonderful histories and fables with their origins in antiquity.

From Asia, for instance, comes a grass seed called Job's tears. These pearly gray seeds are perhaps the most ancient and most commonly used of all the "jewelry plants" in the world. These "beads" were named after Job of the Old Testament. In other parts of the world, they are called "David's tears," "Saint Mary's tears," and "Christ's tears." These seeds, found in jewelry in ancient tombs as well as in today's markets of the Old and New World tropics, grow freely in warm climates, including that of my own back yard. (See the photo on page 39.)

Gallery: *Snuffbox Bean and Sea Heart Jewelry* *by Richard Buckman*

The Mary's bean is the seed of a flowering vine that grows in tropical rain forests of Central and South America. It is named for the Virgin Mary, for it has cross-like indentations in the seed coat. Fable has it that a mother's childbirth pains will be soothed by holding this seed. (See the photo on page 40).

Gallery: *Rose Bead Necklace by Ruth Smith*

Mescal beans were used by Native Americans of the Southwestern United States as a stimulant and hallucinogen in rituals. These bright red, sturdy seeds have been found at burial sites in the Southwest and Mexico as long ago as 1500 B.C. This small tree still grows in Texas and Mexico, and its seeds have long been used to make stunning necklaces. Mescal bean trees can be cultivated in other areas and grown for their striking purple flowers, gray pods, and scarlet seeds. (See the photo on page 49.)

Rose beads, made from molded crushed rose petals, originated in India and were used as prayer beads. Our term "rosary" comes from rose prayer beads adapted for Christian use by Eastern monks in the third century.

Begin Where You Are

Forests, deserts, and seashores aren't the only environments that provide interesting and intriguing plants, animals, and minerals. Once you've become accustomed to observing what's around you, even an urban neighborhood in the largest city can reveal a rich cornucopia of diverse natural wonders that easily rivals the nearest man-made botanical garden or museum.

Gallery: *Tagua Nut Necklace from Ecuador from the collection of Robert Spragg, Sr.*

Take a walk or bicycle ride around your neighborhood and look at what's growing. Think of it as a treasure hunt. It's especially fun if you share your discoveries with interested companions or children. By identifying and reading about the odds and ends you bring back home, you can continue to appreciate and learn about where you've been and where you would like to go next, even if it's just down the road.

Gallery: *Miniature Gourd Mask Pin by Dyan Mai Peterson*

You never know where your curiosity will lead you. Begin by studying just a handful of trees in your area. Follow them through the seasons, learn when they flower, when they produce fruit, nuts, or seeds, and when and if they shed foliage. You may be then inspired to learn about the origin and introduction of foreign trees and shrubs, about world economic botany, endangered plant species, and even about the ocean currents that carry vegetation from the rain forest to distant shores.

If you have the opportunity to travel, use it as a means of expanding your world knowledge of flora and fauna. As a recalcitrant pack rat, I've collected many natural mementos of past adventures—seashells and cuttlefish bones from the Sea of Japan, limpet shells from the coast of Southern California, hemlock cones from the Appalachians, and buckeyes and burdock burrs from Minnesota. These gifts of the earth are more valuable to me than any souvenir I could have purchased.

Gallery: *Shell, Bamboo, and Sea Urchin Spine Necklace by Sharon O'Connell*

How To Use This Book

I have created most of the projects from natural materials that I've gathered myself. While I've described materials many of you will be familiar with, you may need to make substitutions based on your locale. If you're looking for materials that are unavailable in your area, I've included a source list to help you find what you might need.

The chapters on gathering natural materials and growing your own materials give you basic information on what to look for and how to clean and prepare what you find. The materials chapter, which divides the materials used in the projects into geographic location, ecosystem, or cultural reference, offers descriptions and ways to work with specific materials.

Gallery: *Aqua Glass Earrings from the collection of Cathleen Dunne*

If you've never made jewelry before, don't let this deter you from attempting a project. You'll find that reading over the chapter on basic tools and techniques will help you get started. Most of my techniques were developed from my grab-bag of skills, not from any formal training. Look at each project that you make as a valuable experience—practice is essential. Pliers and drills may feel awkward at first, but if you prevail you'll be pleased with the results.

Gallery: *Miniature Vases and plates carved from Tagua Nuts by Robert Spragg, Sr.*

I urge you to consider giving away what you make. Natural jewelry is a way to share your love of the environment and to teach others what you've learned. Also, a handmade object is always a special treat to receive, carrying with it the extra gift of your time and talents.

Gallery: *Tagua Nut Buttons from the collection of Robert Spragg, Sr.*

It's my hope that you'll use the projects in this book as points of departure for your own creativity and curiosity. Have fun creating a unique piece of jewelry, but also spend time learning about things you may not have thought about before. It is this act of discovery, even of such small things as twigs and seeds, that makes this such an exciting pastime.

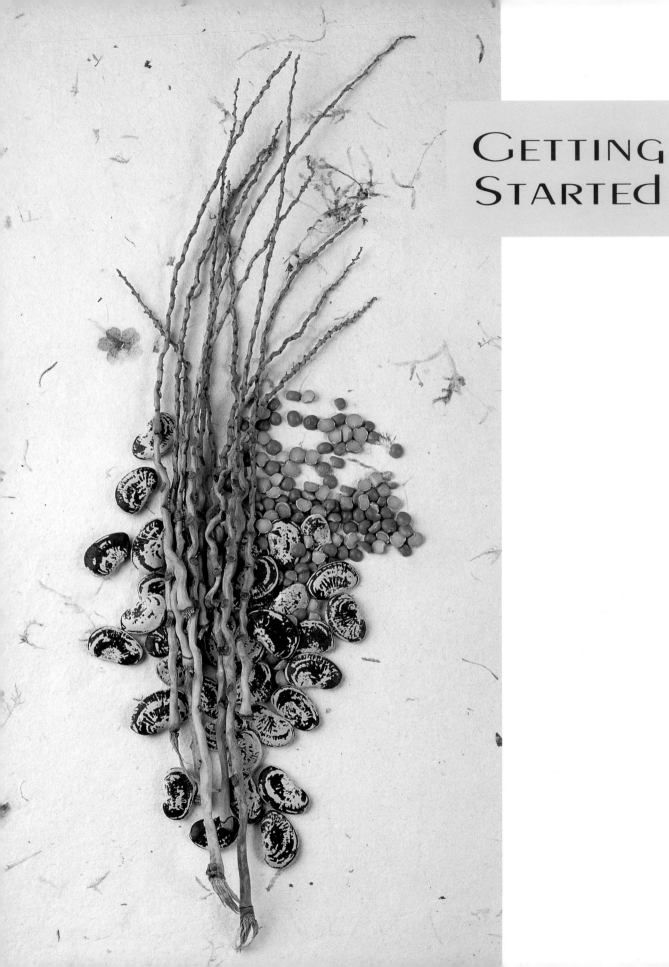

Getting Started

Hunting and Gathering Natural Materials

Finding, identifying, and harvesting materials are my favorite activities in making natural jewelry. Not only do they provide great physical exercise, they provide wonderful mental exercise by sharpening your powers of observation and by expanding your knowledge of the incredible variety of plants that are available for study and use.

The best place to start is just outside your front door. I've found that everyday errands, such as trips to the grocery store or office, are much more pleasurable when I can take a detour to see what's growing on the streets and back alleys of my neighborhood.

Collecting can easily become a year-round activity. You'll need to observe trees and plants during

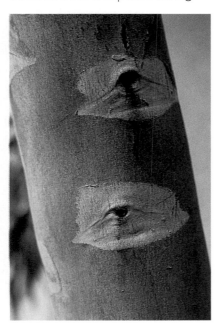

Eucalyptus Bark

different growth and seasonal phases before you can accurately identify them in standard field guides. I've found it helpful to carry a small pocket journal and pencil for noting the location of certain plants as well as information on when they bloom and produce fruit and seeds. I can then return to the same plant when it's time to harvest materials. It's also a good idea to take photographs of certain trees or plants during every season to give you a year-long record of each plant. Then, if you can't find the plant in a field guide, you can take the photographs to a plant nursery or botanist for identification.

Gear

You don't need to spend a fortune outfitting yourself for these expeditions. You may find that you already have many of the items around the house. You may want to keep a backpack or tote bag filled with essential gear, then when the mood strikes, just grab the pack and go. Following are suggestions for simple supplies that will help you when you go out collecting.

For a short walk:
- Sealable plastic bags
- Pocket knife or pruning shears
- Gloves for protection from stickers and irritants
- Camera and film
- Small pocket journal and pencil for notes
- A bucket for specimens too large for plastic bags

For a day outing:
- All the items listed for a short walk, plus . . .
- Suitable clothing for the area and time of year, including a hat, sunglasses, umbrella, and rainwear
- Waterproof boots
- Binoculars
- A bucket with a lid for wet things
- Extension grabber—you can buy these in drugstores and hospital supply stores
- Small ladder
- Field guides

- Pruning saw
- Scissors
- Water—enough for drinking and cleaning up
- Paper towels or other cleanup items
- Snakebite kit
- Insecticide
- Sunscreen
- Flashlight
- Maps (pocket-size, government topographical maps show streams, ponds, and areas of vegetation)
- Old phone books for pressing plants
- Tweezers to remove thorns and splinters
- Compass

Extras that are nice to have:
- A vasculum (this is a specialized container for keeping plants fresh while you're transporting them)
- A plant press

Collecting Etiquette

Here are a few do's and don'ts of collecting that can save you considerable embarassment when you have to explain your numerous bags of nuts, berries, seeds, twigs, and leaves to an irate property owner.

- ❦ Ask property owners for their permission to look at or collect anything.

- ❦ Keep photographs of your natural jewelry with you. It's a lot easier to show property owners what you're doing than it is to explain that you're going to make jewelry out of seeds and twigs.

- ❦ Bring a few samples of your work with you—you never know when you might need to barter for seeds or pods.

- ❦ Carry a name card with you.

- ❦ Know the local environmental laws.

- ❦ On public property, be aware of posted signs that may prohibit removing materials. When you see these warnings, it's best to go elsewhere.

- ❦ Always leave an area as you found it.

- ❦ Consider materials that have fallen on the sidewalk or into the street as fair game, unless you know otherwise.

- ❦ Don't overcollect. It's tempting to take more than you need.

What to Do When You Can't Find the Materials You Need

Since some of the plant and animal materials listed in the projects may not be indigenous to your area, you won't be able to personally collect all the materials you need. You may also want to create your own designs with materials that are not readily available or that come from exotic habitats. On pages 123-124 you'll find a source list that will help you locate any materials you'll need for completing these projects or for experimenting with your own designs.

Cleaning and Preparation

Once you've collected your materials, you'll need to make sure they're clean and free of vermin. First, divide the materials into two groups: sturdy materials, such as twigs and large seeds that can tolerate rough cleaning; and fragile materials, such as papery seed pods that can tolerate only a gentle rinsing.

Mescal Beans Pods

To remove dust and dirt, place the materials in a colander and rinse them with water. To keep bugs out of your house, it's best to wash everything outside using a garden hose. You may want to keep several colanders on hand just for this purpose. Other handy cleaning supplies are scrub brushes, liquid dish soap, a bucket, old toothbrushes, cotton swabs, pipe cleaners, bottle brushes, and toothpicks to clean nooks and crannies. And don't forget rubber gloves to protect your hands. It's also helpful to have acetone (fingernail polish remover) on hand to remove sticky substances, such as sap and other plant resins.

Chinaberry Tree

After the initial rinsing, examine the materials closely for stubborn dirt. To remove this from sturdy materials, use a scrub brush or old toothbrush with liquid dish soap. For fragile materials, soak them clean in water and liquid dish soap.

If you need to remove flesh from seeds, hold them under running water and remove as much as you can with your fingers first. Then scrub the seeds or pits with an old toothbrush and liquid dish soap. Don't be discouraged if you can't remove all the fleshy matter; let the seeds or pits dry, then use an abrasive material, such as steel wool or sandpaper, to remove any remaining matter.

You can also use a rock tumbler to remove stubborn plant matter from seeds. Tumble hard, sturdy seeds with water and coarse silicon-carbide grit (#60) for a day or so. Tumble fragile seeds with silicon-carbide grit alone, noting that tumbling without water will take longer.

Pindo Palm

Dry the washed materials in the sun by laying them out on old towels or paper towels in your back yard or on a windowsill. If your space is tight, consider using a food dehydrator to dry materials quickly and conveniently. This is especially helpful during rainy spells or if you live in a humid climate. Place the materials to be dried on the dehydrator's trays and adjust the heat to be as low as possible. Check the items frequently to make sure they are not being damaged by the heat.

When the materials are clean and dry, check them for external signs of insect infestation by carefully examining them for small holes, indentations, and powdery residue. Seeds and plant parts that do not show signs of infestation may still harbor unseen embryonic bugs that can hatch inside the material. To keep bugs out of your jewelry, disinfect all raw material by freezing them after they have been cleaned and dried.

To do this, place a layer of materials on a paper plate or tray, then cover the materials with wax paper. Continue to layer the materials, separating each layer with wax paper, then place them in your freezer for a minimum of three days. If the materials are large or thick, freeze them for at least five days. The more time in the freezer, the better. Hint: If you don't have time to clean raw materials as soon as you've brought them home, freeze them in airtight containers until you can clean them.

After freezing, thaw the materials, dry them if necessary, and store them in airtight containers

such as sealable plastic bags, or canning jars. Be sure you label all materials; it's easy to forget what you've collected, especially after they've spent a few days in cold storage. Bones, feathers, horn, and teeth, will not attract vermin if they are immaculately clean. Make sure they've been scrubbed, dried, and disinfected by freezing; they do not require airtight storage.

Beautiful But Deadly— Poisonous Materials

Many plant materials historically used for jewelry are toxic. When you go into the field you will need to be able to identify them. Refer to a field guide for information on plant toxicity. If you do use materials that are toxic, be aware of what you're handling and keep these materials out of the reach of children and animals.

Know that almost any substance can be considered poisonous in certain quantities, so heed these words of warning—avoid ingesting any material not specifically deemed as food. Even then, you must be careful; nutmeg, for example, is a wonderful spice but is toxic when ingested in unusual quantities.

Take time to preview the materials used in this book to be sure that you do not have allergies to any of them. Be aware that you can have allergic reactions to materials that touch the skin or that are inhaled. Below are the descriptions of some toxic seeds that are commonly used in jewelry.

Precatory Beans (*Abrus precatorius*) are striking red and black seeds. Though beautiful, they are not used in this book. The inside of the tough, smooth seed is highly toxic—one seed can kill a person. While they are used in many countries for jewelry, these tropical seeds have been banned from import into the United States.

Castor Bean (*Ricin communis*) is the source of commercial castor oil, but the raw substance contained in all parts of the plant is a deadly toxin. The seeds contain the poison ricin, which has been used in poisoned darts. *Ricin* is from Latin, meaning tick, which the seed resembles. The plant is an annual and is often grown as an ornamental. You may also find it growing on undeveloped land, having escaped from cutivation.

Oleander (*Nerium oleander*) and **Yellow Oleander**, also called lucky nut (*Thevetia peruviana*), contain toxins in all parts of the plant. Do not even burn these plants, as inhalation of the smoke can cause poisoning.

Mescal Beans (*Sophora secundiflora*), also called Texas mountain laurel, are the attractive seeds of a small tree and can cause hallucinations, lethargy, and death when ingested. Make sure you keep these seeds away from children. (See the photo on page 14.)

Nutmeg (*Myristica fragrans*), used sparingly as a culinary spice, is perfectly safe. But in large quantities, nutmeg can cause nausea, vomiting, and possibly death.

Moonflower (*Calonyction aculeatum*) and **Morning Glory** (*Ipomea* spp.) contain chemicals that can be extracted and made into LSD. Fortunately, commercial morning glory seeds are treated so that LSD cannot be synthesized from them. Do not ingest any of these seeds.

BOTANICAL NAMES

Classified plants and animals have both common names and scientific names. Common names are given to plants by people who are familiar with them. The same plant may be known by many different common names around the world. However, a plant can only have one scientific name, which has been assigned to it and maintained by agreement among the worldwide scientific community.

The scientific name is always italicized in text. It consists of at least two Latinized words. The first term is the genus name and is, by convention, always capitalized; the second term, never capitalized, is the species name and is a subcategory of the genus.

As an example, the plant whose common name is Job's tears has as its scientific name *Coix lacryma-jobi*. *Coix* is the genus name and may be assigned to other plants that share specific characteristics with Job's Tears. The species name, *lacryma-jobi*, is assigned only to Job's Tears. No other plant can share these two terms, which allows for people of different cultures and languages to have a standardized name to which only Job's tears is assigned.

Growing Your Own Materials

You'll find that growing your own materials is endlessly entertaining. At first, it may seem a bit odd to go out in your garden and pick jewelry parts off trees and shrubs. Over time, though, you'll come to appreciate the fun of planting seeds or small plants, watching them grow to decorate your yard, then harvesting their bits and pieces for raw materials.

If your climate isn't suited for warm-weather vegetation, consider planting in pots; you can then protect your plants during the winter by sheltering them in your garage or house. While a greenhouse is an ideal factory for natural beads, a warm spot with sufficient artificial light will keep many sun-loving plants thriving until they return to the outdoors.

If you do decide to try your hand at some of the more unusual plants listed in this book, such as rain forest plants, read everything you can about their natural habitat and environmental needs. And keep in mind the time a plant takes to mature, flower, and fruit. While tamarind seeds would be wonderful to harvest from your own tree, you'll need to put this project on hold for a few years before your tree bears its first bean pod. In this chapter, I've included a few plants that produce harvestable jewelry materials in a short time, many within the first season of growth.

Balloon Vines (*Cardiospermum halicacabum*), also called heartseed, have green paperlike seed pods that are balloon-shaped; each pod is approximately 1 inch (2.5 cm) in diameter. Inside each pod is a small, hard, round seed with a whitish heart-shaped spot. The pods appear in late summer or early fall.

Where I live, balloon vines grow without support in the wild in parks and wastelands. Their long stems often cover the grass and weeds along roadsides and pathways. These vines can also be trained upward on a support or trellis and can be grown as an annual in cooler areas (zones 4 to 8) or as a perennial in warmer areas (zones 9 to 10).

To grow them, soak the seeds overnight in warm water before planting either indoors in peat-pots in late winter, or outdoors after all danger of frost has passed. They do not transplant well, so plant them in a permanent place, setting the seedlings or seeds 12 to 18 inches (30.5-45.5 cm) apart and provide them with a support for climbing. Harvest the seeds in the fall, when the pods have turned brown.

Bamboo (*Phyllostachys* spp.) is wonderful to have in your yard or garden, but heed this warning: once you plant bamboo, you'll have it forever—and you may have much, much more than you ever wanted. Many bamboos spreads rapidly underground by producing new culms (stalks). If you don't control it, it will take over your garden. To grow bamboo, it's best to contact a professional bamboo grower who can help you choose one of the many varieties available.

Purchase live plants, and make sure that you know whether the variety you choose is a clumping variety or a running variety. Clumping bamboo sends up new culms from a central root cluster, while running bamboo sends out runners that can quickly turn a few shoots into a forest if left untended. You can contain bamboo's growth by either planting it in large pots or by sinking a piece of metal sheeting deep around the perimeter of its outdoor growing area.

Harvest the culms whenever you wish. You may leave them outdoors to dry, which will yield somewhat brittle brown canes. Or, cut the culms and use them

Bamboo

wet and green. Bamboo cut at this time will maintain its green color for a very long time before it fades to a soft cream color. See page 38 for more information on bamboo.

Beans (*Phaseolus* spp.) are fast growers, making them a perfect project for children and adults who like quick results. You can plant them every two weeks during their growing season to ensure a continuous and ample harvest. And, if you have an overabundance, you can always dry and store the beans for later use.

In growing beans, you must first choose between bush or pole beans. Then, you must choose among the many varieties in each of these categories. If you grow beans specifically for jewelry making, choose colorful and interesting ones, such as black-and-white calypso beans. See page 43 for more information on beans.

Cannas (*Canna* spp.) are easy to grow and easy to keep, especially in warm climates where they can be left in the ground over the win-

Canna pods

ter. They thrive in warm, sunny locations and prefer damp soil. You can buy canna plants, or you can raise them from seed. Either way, they are fast growers and prolific seed bearers. Make sure that the variety you plant will bear the kind of seeds you want. Some cannas produce round seeds, some oval, and some none at all since some hybrids are sterile. Check with your seed supplier or nursery about specific varieties. Plant them early in the spring and then just wait for the seeds to develop. My experience is that they grow quickly and produce seeds starting in midsummer.

To grow cannas from seed, soak the seeds overnight in warm water. Then either plant them in peat pots indoors during the winter, placing the seeds approximately ½ inch (1.5 cm) deep in rich potting soil, or, plant the seeds directly outdoors as soon as danger of frost has past. Cannas multiply quickly and like lots of room, so consider these characteristics in choosing their growing location. Harvest canna seeds when the seed pods are brown and papery. See page 41 for more information on cannas.

Chinese Wisteria (*Wisteria chinensis*) is easy to grow from seed, although you may have to wait several seasons before your new plant blooms and seeds. In early spring, this deciduous plant produces fragrant purple or white flowers. In late summer, it produces velvety green seed pods that mature and harden in the fall. Each of these pods contains flat brown seeds.

This plant can be grown in zones 5 to 9 as a strong, heavy, woody vine, as a shrub, or

Chinese wisteria pods

trained as a tree. Be aware that wisteria cultivated as vines produces strong and heavy vines that can pull down less-than-sturdy supports. It can also be grown in a container.

Wisteria is readily available at plant nurseries, or it can be grown from seed. To grow from seed, either plant the seeds indoors in pots in the winter or outside in full sun after the last frost, keeping the soil moist until the seed germinates. See pages 38-39 for more information on Chinese Wisteria.

Gourds come in three varieties: the Cucurbita (*Cucurbita* spp.), or ornamental; the Laginaria (*Laginaria* spp.), or hardshell; and the Luffa (*Luffa* spp.), or vegetable sponge. The most common gourd used for decorating is the laginaria.

The blossoms of the plant are white and bloom at night. The gourds are green and need plenty of sun, space, and water as they grow. Plant the seeds in full sun after all danger of frost is past. The gourds grow on vines that can be trained on a trellis. If you want perfect specimens, you may need to make a support sling to keep the gourds off the ground as they grow.

Because the gourds have a thick, hard shell, and are 90 to 95% water, they may take six months to a year to dry after you harvest them before making them into jewelry. Though the gourds may look rather ugly when dried—dirty, moldy, and gray—you can easily prepare them for decorating with a firm but gentle cleaning using a stiff brush and warm water. Cut the clean, dried gourd using a

Job's tears

motorized craft saw, remove the seeds inside, then cut smaller shapes from the shell for your jewelry. The small mini-gourd varieties can be used to make round earrings and pendants. (See the projects on page 106.)

Job's Tears (*Coix lacryma-jobi*) is an annual grass that looks like growing corn, and can grow to 10 feet (3 m) in height. It's an easy plant to cultivate and will produce profuse seeds in one season. In warm climates, you can leave the plant in the ground over the winter; the next spring it will send up more stalks and produce even more seeds. In cooler climates, you'll need to replant either seeds or the previous year's tubers. If you plant from seed, make sure the seeds are fresh and viable; consider ordering them from a seed supplier for planting purposes.

In early spring, plant the seeds approximately ½ inch (1.5 cm) deep in peat pots filled with moist potting soil. When the weather's warm enough, move them outdoors. Seeds will appear in the late summer or fall, following the plant's lush vegetative growth of leaves. The seeds start out green, then turn to black, then pearly gray, and finally to white. Pick the seeds when they are black or gray. If you wait too long and let them turn white, they tend to shrivel when dried. See page 39 for more information on Job's tears.

Lotus (*Nelumbo nucifera*, *Nelumbo lutea*, and other species) thrives in marsh, swamp, or pond environments. Aside from producing jewelry material, it is a useful plant to

grow. Almost the entire plant is edible, including the roots, leaves, and seeds.

If you plan on growing more than a few plants in a natural setting, check with local environmentalists—a small ecosystem can be profoundly affected by the introduction of new vegetation. If you don't have a wet area near you, you can grow lotus plants in a large tub or container—or use it as an excuse to finally build your own garden pond for growing aquatic plants. Lotus plants are hardy in zones 4 to 10 and thrive in full sun.

To grow lotus, you can purchase either plants or seeds. To plant the seeds, roll them in clay to weight them, then drop them into the pond. Check to make sure you know the maximum depth at which the plants or seeds can be planted. To grow them in a container, mix 8 to 16 ounces (227-454 g) of commercial aquatic plant fertilizer with water in a 10 gallon (35 L) container. Plant as above, then follow the fertilizer's instructions for feeding the plants once a month during the growing season. Flowers appear in mid- to late summer. When the seeds turn brown and woody, usually during the fall they are ready to harvest. See page 40 for more information on lotus.

Melons and Squash (members of the *Cucurbita* family) are easy to germinate, fast growing, and quick to flower and fruit. If you have a small yard or garden, you can grow them vertically on a fence or trellis. Since cantaloupe, honeydew melon, watermelon, and squash are grown from seed, you can purchase seeds or save seeds from melons and squash you've purchased from the grocery store. Just make sure you don't plant seedless varieties if you are planning to harvest jewelry materials!

Plant melons or squash outdoors in the spring. Make small mounds of garden soil, planting several seeds in each mound. Then, keep the soil damp until the leaves pop up. Don't plant different melons and squash close to each other; they can cross-pollinate to produce some very odd and unappetizing fruit. See page 44 for more information on melons and squash.

Moonflowers (*Calonyction aculeatum*) are plants with lovely twining vines, similar to morning glory vines, except that they have

large white flowers that bloom at dusk and stay fragrantly open during the night and into the morning hours. Its genus name, calonyction, means "beautiful night." A fast grower, it can climb 10 feet (3 m) or more in a single season, so you'll need a support for the vines that is about 10 feet (3 m) tall.

Before planting, soak the seeds overnight in warm water. Then either plant them in peat pots eight weeks before the last predicted frost, or plant the seeds directly in the ground in average garden soil after the last frost of the winter. Space the seedlings or seeds 9 to 12 inches (23-30.5 cm) apart. This vine is considered perennial in warm climates, zones 9 to 10, and an annual in zones 3 to 8.

At the end of the growing season, in late summer or early fall, the vines will produce capsules containing seeds. Simply remove the seeds when they are mature (the pods will be brown and crisp) and let them dry before using them for jewelry making. See page 30 for more information on moonflowers.

Basic Tools and Techniques

The following lists include all the tools, assembly materials, and miscellaneous supplies that you'll need to make the projects in this book. Note that these are general lists; each individual project lists specific tools and materials. If you do basic craft work or make jewelry, you may already have most of these items. All the power tools listed are optional, since you can make all the jewelry with hand tools. However, I recommend purchasing some or all of these power tools; once you're comfortable using them, you'll save time when performing repetitive tasks, giving you more time for improving your skills. A few of these tools may be new to you—rock tumblers and craft drills for instance—and are discussed in detail below.

Clockwise from top: Clamps; jeweler's rouge—paste and cake; jeweler's cloth; sandpaper; file; assorted pliers; crimping pliers, center front; wire cutters

Pliers and Holding Devices

- 2 pairs of flat-nose pliers, one with smooth jaws, one with serrated jaws
- Round-nose pliers
- Needle-nose pliers with serrated jaws
- Crimping pliers
- Standard pliers
- Vise (a small tabletop vise is sufficient)
- Clamps (C-clamps, spring clamps, binder clips, paper clips)
- String for binding
- Binding wire (inexpensive soft wire)
- Rubber bands

Sanding and Polishing Equipment

- Abrasive wheels to fit craft drill
- Sandpaper in coarse grit (#60-#150), medium grit (#200-#400), and fine grit (#600)
- Sanding barrels in various grits to fit craft drill
- Buffing wheels to fit craft drill
- Jeweler's rouge
- Lint-free cotton rags for hand buffing
- Jeweler's polishing cloth (this is impregnated on one side with jeweler's rouge)
- Rock tumbler and barrels
- Silicon-carbide grit for rock tumbler (grades #60, #100, #200, #400)
- Rouge-coated crushed walnut shells (polishing compound) for use in rock tumbler
- Spray lacquer, varnish, or clear enamel
- Furniture wax

Cutting Tools

- Wire cutters (light and heavy duty)
- Scissors
- Hacksaw with blades
- Fine-tooth model-making saws
- Pruning shears
- Saw blades and cutoff wheels to fit a motorized craft drill
- Craft knife with disposable blades (#11 is a good general blade), or good carving knife

Piercing and Drilling Tools

- Motorized craft drill with attachments
- Power drill
- Drill bits—at least one 1/16-inch (.6 cm) bit and one 1/32-inch (.8 cm) bit (a set of graduated bits is a good investment)
- Set of numbered drill bits, sizes #61-#80
- 1/2 inch (1 cm) in diameter plug cutters
- Diamond-coated drill bits for cutting glass, shell, stone, and other hard materials
- Shallow can (a cat food can works best)

Adhesives and Gluing Accessories

- Two-part epoxy glue
- Strong, quick-drying glue
- 1/2-inch (1.5-cm) masking tape
- White clear-drying craft glue
- Wax paper
- Toothpicks or twigs for mixing epoxy
- Acetone or glue remover for removing quick-drying glue

Jewelry Findings and Materials

- Jump rings
- Ear wires or backs
- Chain
- Beading thread
- Cording (hemp, jute, leather)
- Jewelry wire
- Tigertail
- Memory wire
- Clasps
- Spacers
- Crimp beads
- Crimp ends
- Spacer beads

- Head pins
- Eye pins
- Pin backs
- Hair clips
- Clear nylon thread or fishing line

Miscellaneous Tools and Equipment

- Safety goggles
- Dust mask
- Ruler
- Tape measure
- Drawing templates (circles, squares, triangles, etc.)
- Black felt-tipped pen
- India ink and pen (to sign your work)
- Wood-burning tool (optional)
- Plastic putty
- Tapestry needle for cord and raffia
- Sewing needle to fit beading thread
- Metallic gold pen

Some Notes on Tools

The best general advice I can give is to buy the best tools you can afford, and keep them cleaned and lubricated. Well-made and well-maintained tools will endure years of hard service. Make sure the pliers you buy are sturdy and comfortable to your grip. Always use sharp and straight drill bits and blades; dull ones are unsafe and inefficient.

Motorized craft drills are designed for the craftsman who produces small or finely detailed pieces. I've found them to be indispensable—I keep two handy, each with a different accessory attached. Several manufacturers make these tools, each of which offers a variety of accessories, such as collets and mandrels, aluminum-oxide abrasive wheels, sanding disks and drums, felt and cotton buffing wheels, saw blades, and cutting wheels.

Rock tumblers are used to smooth and polish rocks and minerals. They can also polish seeds and frost and smooth bottle glass. The machine consists of a motor, a frame with axles, and containers (barrels). The motor constantly rotates one or more of the sealed rubber barrels that are filled with raw material, water, and an abrasive to make the material smooth and shiny. While not an essential piece of equipment, a rock tumbler is fun to use and is necessary for polishing large quantities of material at one time.

Rock tumbler and motorized craft drill with assorted drill bits and attachments
The numbered drill bits and diamond-coated drill bit are shown at the center front

Working Techniques

Once you've cleaned and disinfected your materials (see pages 14-15), you will need to prepare them to become the individual components for your project. Below, I've provided general instructions for basic techniques. However, keep in mind that different materials might call for different preparation based on the material's composition. The materials section and the project instructions will give you specific information about working with individual materials.

Drilling

Drilling holes in small, irregularly shaped objects may be new to you. While it takes a bit of patience and practice, it's an easy skill to learn. To drill materials, you'll need a motorized craft drill or an electric drill, a drill bit, and a clamp or vise to hold the material to be drilled.

For making jewelry, you'll need drill bits that make holes small enough for threading head pins and wire. I most often use bits that are $\frac{3}{32}$ inch (.2 cm) in diameter and smaller. Bits ranging from $\frac{1}{4}$ to $\frac{1}{32}$ inch (.5- .08 cm) are often sold in sets and are a good investment if you buy the best quality that you can afford. Smaller drill bits are called "numbered" drills and can usually be purchased in sets in sizes #61-#80.

Until you've had plenty of practice, hold pieces to be drilled in a vise, being careful when tightening the jaws to avoid cracking the material. I have found, after much experimentation, that

You can transform just about any raw material into a bead with the right drilling tool

holding materials with my thumb and forefinger is quicker and more efficient than drilling materials held in a vise. However, be forewarned: it takes quite a bit of dexterity, as well as a few minor wounds, to get good at this.

For tough seeds, always make sure you start with a sharp drill bit. You will need to introduce the drill bit to each seed gently and patiently. Hard, shiny seeds are often difficult to drill through; the drill bit may "skate" on the surface of the seed instead of starting a hole. Examine each seed for flat spots or indentations where you can begin drilling. Touch the spinning bit lightly to the seed until you feel the bit make contact with and grab hold of the surface, known as to "find

purchase." If you force the bit, it will skitter across the surface.

DRILLING HARD MATERIALS

For drilling glass, pebbles, seashells, and other hard or thick materials, you'll need to use a diamond-coated drill bit for your craft drill. You can buy either a solid-core (sintered) bit made of a solid conglomeration of diamond chips, or a metal bit that has been coated with diamond chips. Both use industrial-grade diamonds and cost just a little more than standard bits.

Since diamond bits cut by abrasion, you will need to irrigate the drilling site with water to remove debris from the hole as you drill. The easiest way that I've found to do this is to first place a piece of plastic putty in the bottom of a shallow can (a cat food can is ideal). Next, firmly stick the material to be drilled to the putty; this will prevent the material from moving as you drill. Then, pour enough water into the can to just cover both the putty and the material. Using a sharp, narrow diamond bit on your drill, and holding the can steady with your free hand, introduce the spinning bit to the material, drilling through the water.

As soon as you have a hole started, exert just enough downward pressure on the bit to keep it in the hole. Lift the bit every one or two seconds to allow the bit and the material to cool, and to allow the debris to exit the hole. Do not exert heavy pressure or you may overheat the bit, which will break the material. Keep drilling, alternately lifting and inserting the bit, until the hole goes through to the

other side. Then, turn the piece over and drill through from the other side. If the hole is not big enough, enlarge it using a slightly larger bit.

CUTTING

At times, you'll need to cut, whittle, or saw raw materials. When working on small, intricate materials, use handsaws for slow, careful cutting. I use a hacksaw with fine-tooth blades, a craft knife with coarse- and fine-tooth saw blades, a jeweler's saw, and cut-off wheels and rotary saw blades for my craft drill. I've also found that scissors and wire cutters can come in handy. If you plan on doing a great deal of cutting and have an adequate work area, you might want to invest in a band saw with fine-tooth blades.

For whittling and trimming, I use a craft knife with disposable blades. These sharp blades are perfect for shaving off excess dried glue and close trimming of bamboo and twigs. You may want to experiment with the different cutting blades available for craft knives.

Saws are particularly dangerous. Make sure you know all safety precautions before using. Be especially careful when using the rotary saw blades for your craft drill. These blades are very sharp. When running at high speed, they can be very hard to control until you've had some practice using them. Make sure you follow the manufacturer's instructions for choosing the proper speed for using these blades. In general, when using a rotary saw blade, hold the material in a vise and keep both hands on the drill at all times.

It's always best to practice first on scrap materials until you feel comfortable.

SANDING AND GRINDING

The specific materials you use will determine whether you will sand by hand or by power. Generally, hard materials, such as coconut shell, palm seeds, and tagua nuts, can tolerate being sanded by power. More delicate or intricate materials, such as seed pods, nutmeg slices, and black walnut slices, require slow, careful sanding by hand.

To accommodate all materials, you should have various grades of sandpaper as well as sanding accessories for a craft drill available. You'll need sandpaper in three grades: coarse (#60-#150), medium (#200-#400), and fine (#600). Note that using wet/dry sandpaper will create less dust. When sanding with a craft drill, you'll need coarse, medium, and fine sanding barrels and sanding disks.

When working with metal, you'll need a grinding wheel attachment for your craft drill. The Stippled Sea Heart (see page 56), for example, requires that metal head pins be ground flush with the sea heart's surface. Make sure to check the user's manual for your power tool for the right speed to use with grinding wheels. Also, use safety goggles and a dust mask to protect your eyes, nose, and mouth from the fine metal particles that come from grinding.

GLUING

You will need three kinds of glue for the projects in this book: two-part epoxy which requires mixing; strong quick-drying glue; and white clear-drying craft glue. Keep wax paper and toothpicks or twigs handy for mixing epoxy. Place glued pieces on wax paper while they harden. Use all glues sparingly, and keep paper towels or rags close by to remove any drips or blobs. Once dried, use a sharp craft knife to shave off any excess glue.

POLISHING

Various materials require different kinds of polishing and buffing. Many seeds and plant materials have their own natural wax coating to protect them from desiccation or moisture invasion and require only buffing to achieve a nice finish. When working with new or unfamiliar materials, I buff them a bit to see if they will polish up on their own. Before polishing, make sure items are completely free of scratches, abrasions, and rough areas. In general, thoroughly sand them by hand or abrade them in a rock tumbler to a good matte finish.

To polish using a craft drill, use a cloth or felt buffing wheel. Touch the spinning wheel a few times to jeweler's rouge, which comes in either a cake or paste. Apply the wheel to the piece, holding it to the surface just a little longer than you think may be necessary to get a good finish. Be careful to protect your eyes and face, since cloth polishing wheels can spin off loose threads.

To buff using a craft drill, use a clean polishing wheel without rouge to remove excess rouge and produce a nice shine. Keep the rouge-filled wheel aside—you can use it several times before discarding it. You can also polish by hand, using a jeweler's polishing cloth which you can find at jewelry stores or through jewelry supply companies. To buff by hand, use a soft, lint-free cloth.

To polish materials in a rock tumbler, make sure the materials are completely free of grit. Then tumble them with crushed walnut shells that have been coated with jeweler's rouge. You can buy crushed walnut shells already filled with rouge at a lapidary- or jewelry-supply shop.

VARNISHING AND LACQUERING

I prefer leaving materials with their natural finish or with the polished and buffed finish described above. While lacquer, varnish, or clear enamel can add shine to dull materials, they can eventually peel off. They can also change the color of the materials by darkening them or turning them yellow over time.

Materials that benefit from a coat or two of spray enamel are seeds with thin flaky coats such as calypso beans and soy beans. If you have any doubts, it's always best to perform a test to make sure the finish will adhere to the materials.

To apply, first place the materials on wax paper to prevent them from sticking, next spray or paint, then allow them to dry completely. When working with any of these preparations, particularly in spray form, always make sure you have adequate ventilation.

Assembly

Once the materials are prepared, you're ready to assemble your jewelry. The tools you'll need to do this are round-nose pliers for making loops, two pairs of flat-nose pliers—one with smooth jaws, one with serrated jaws—to hold and manipulate wire, crimping pliers for crushing crimps, and wire cutters. Occasionally you'll find that needle-nose pliers with serrated jaws come in handy, since their long pointed jaws can get into very small spaces.

Using Jewelry Findings

You'll need to become familiar with basic jewelry findings. These are the bits of hardware that hold jewelry components together such as jump rings, head pins, pin backs, crimp ends, bead caps and ends, clasps, and earring hoops, wires, and backs. You can purchase findings at craft-supply stores, bead shops, or through jewelry-supply catalogs. If you've never worked with findings, spend a short time browsing the shops and you will be an expert in no time.

In order to string seeds and beads, you will be using jewelry wire, chain, cord, beading wire (tigertail), and beading thread (on a needle). Beading thread can be made of heavy cotton or synthetics. To support heavier materials, use beading wire. One variety, known as tigertail, is a steel-wrapped thread that is both strong and flexible. Using cords of leather, hemp, twine, cotton, or silk for stringing materials will provide a range of design possibilities for your jewelry.

Wire can serve as a construction material or decorative embellishment. It comes in many sizes, or gauges, and in many different metals. The lower the gauge number, the larger the wire's diameter. You can purchase wire in bead shops or jewelry-supply stores. I've also found many unusual and interesting wires in hardware stores.

Head pins, and dangle pins are short pieces of wire which resemble fat needles, and are used for stringing a selection of beads together. Head pins have flat bottoms that act as stoppers for the beads, while dangle pins have flattened, decorative ends that serve as their stoppers.

A jump ring is a small circle of metal with an opening on its circumference. It's a connector between jewelry components that provides an extra link for strength while adding movement to necklaces and earrings. To attach a jump ring, always open it sideways and close it sideways. If you pull it open and push it

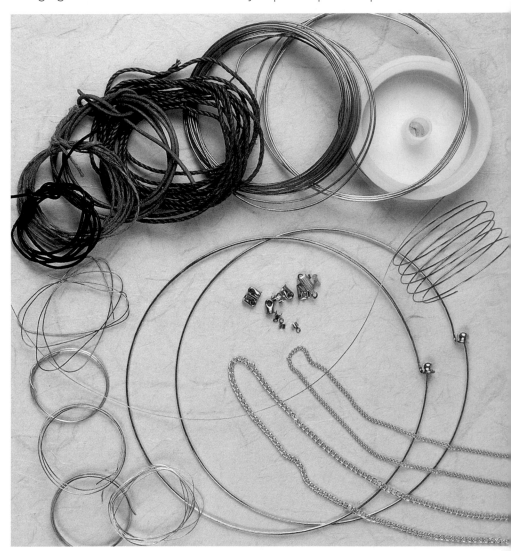

Clockwise from upper left: Assorted cords; copper and silver wire; tigertail; bracelet memory wire; necklace hoops; chain; assorted jewelry wire; and assorted clasps

closed, it will loose its spring and may open at the wrong time.

Ends are used for finishing off a string of beads. Crimp ends (which fold over) and crimp beads (which thread on) fit over the ends of cord, thread, or beading wire to either finish or secure the ends of these materials, or act as stops for other beads. Once they're in place, you will need to use crimping pliers to crush them so they will securely grip the cord or wire.

Bead caps and bead ends hide the knot in the thread or wire. Since they have a built-in loop, you can also glue materials to them to make an instant dangle.

MAKING A LOOP

Once you've strung your material on wire or pins, you'll need to make a loop on the end of the wire for hanging pendants, earrings, or dangles, or for attaching other findings. This is the assembly technique you will perform most often.

To make a loop, grip the wire with the round-nose pliers approximately ½ inch (1.5 cm) from its free end. Wrap the wire end around one jaw of the pliers until you've made a complete circle. Then, with the smooth-jaw, flat-nose pliers, hold the loop flat. With your other hand and the serrated-jaw pliers, wind the wire end tightly and evenly around the shaft of the pin or wire until you run out of wire. With the smooth-jaw, flat-nose pliers, squeeze the wire end tightly to the shaft. Finish by inserting one of the jaws of the round-nose pliers into the loop to round it out and bend it so that it sits centered above the wire shaft.

You can also make a loop in the free end of the wire without wrapping the ends around the shaft. Just cut off any excess wire, leaving enough on the end to make the loop; then use the round-nose pliers as above to shape the loop. This loop is not as secure as the wrapped loop and will not tolerate heavy materials or stress.

Jewelry Findings clockwise, from the left: spring clasps and jump rings; barrette backs; spacer bars; hook-and-eye clasps; bar-and-loop toggle clasp; head pins and dangle pins; pin backs; earring hoops, backs, and wires; assorted beads; crimps; bails

NATIVE AMERICAN

When harvesting your own raw materials for jewelry, you may soon find that much of the "native" vegetation is not actually native at all. Dating from the first settlers of North America, people have brought plants from around the globe to these shores. It has become a bit of a sleuthing game to find out what plants have been here since the recording of flora and fauna began. And in return for my efforts, I have discovered wonderful materials and fascinating information about their cultural and medical importance to the native cultures of North America.

Palmettos provided food for the Florida Seminole Indians; the mescal beans of the Southwest served as a ritual hallucinogen for Native Americans of that area and have been found in Trans-Pecos rock shelters dating from 8400 B.C.; and black walnut hulls and shells have been used for dyeing fibers.

Offered here are only a few of the native plants that I've used in making natural jewelry. I urge you to do some detective work of your own to find out what is native to your area and how it has been used in different North American cultures.

Acorns (*Quercus* spp.) come from the 70 species of oak trees native to the United States, and from about 70 hybrids (mixes of different species). There are oak trees for just about any region or climate. Acorns are available in most parts of the country from late August to early December. Some acorns are edible—those from white oaks, chestnut oaks, and post oak. But before you consider eating them, make sure you are thoroughly familiar with the acorns you collect, for some are bitter and toxic. Acorns are great for children to collect and learn about. While you're making beads, put one or two acorns in a pot with soil or in your garden and let it become a tree; they germinate easily.

To prepare acorns for jewelry making, first check each acorn for cracks or abrasions. If you notice any splits in the shell, don't use it—this is an indication that it has started to germinate. Next, simply wash the acorns well, let them drain and dry on paper towels or in a food dehydrator, then freeze them for three days to kill any embryonic vermin. Drill acorns from the flat top to the bottom, or sideways. You can leave them in their natural state or stain them with leather dye, and you can polish them with jeweler's rouge using a buffing cloth or wheel. You can also use the acorn caps on their own for stringing; some, however, are fragile and must be handled carefully. (See the projects on pages 47 and 69).

Bagpod Trees (*Glottidium vesicarium*) are small, weedy trees native to wastelands of the southeastern United States. Look for these trees with mimosa-like leaves and yellow flowers in pastures and woodlands. In the fall, the trees produce soft, lime-green pods containing hard green seeds that sometimes turn a copper color over time. (See the project on page 77.)

Black Walnuts (*Juglans nigra*) have a thick, hard, furrowed shell and a rich, oily nut inside. You can harvest black walnuts from September to November. While the shell is difficult to cut, you will be rewarded for your efforts when you cut cross-sections to make intricately patterned slices that can be sanded and polished to make attractive jewelry.

To slice a black walnut, place it securely in a vise, and cut crosswise with a fine-tooth saw blade. If you plan to make more than a few slices, you might want to invest in or borrow a band saw, using a fine-tooth blade for cutting. Watch your fingers; it's difficult to cut round or irregularly shaped objects on a band saw. Make each slice a little less than ¼ inch (.5 cm) thick; any thinner and the slices may break. Sand the sections first with medium-grit (#200) sandpaper, then with progressively finer grits. Coat the slices with furniture wax and buff them with a jeweler's polishing cloth or buffing wheel. To make a pendant or earrings from a slice, drill a hole through the top of the flat face of the slice. Attach one or more jump rings, then a chain or cord for a pendant, or earring findings of your choice. (See the projects on page 110).

Hackberry (*Celtis occidentalis* and other species) comes in several varieties that are all native to North America. Hackberry trees are fast growing and have deep roots that will not interfere with surface structures, such as sidewalks, so they are often planted along city streets. These trees are easily identified by their warty bark. Hackberry trees produce small berries in profusion that attract and feed birds. The berries can be picked, dried, and drilled to use as beads. When dried and shriveled, the berries make attractive beads with an interesting texture. Harvest hackberry fruit from late summer to December. (See the project on page 54.)

Jojoba
(*Simmondsia chinensis*) is an evergreen shrub indigenous to the Sonoran Desert of the United States and Northwestern Mexico. Its attractive seeds contain oil that is extracted to produce jojoba oil, a luxurious oil used as substitute for sperm whale oil in the cosmetics industry. The oil is also used as an industrial lubricant. To make beads, drill the seeds lengthwise or crosswise. (See the project on page 80.)

Kentucky Coffee Tree
(*Gymnocladus dioica*) produces large, sturdy bean pods filled with brown seeds that are round and almost flat. Historians tell us that the seeds were roasted by Civil War soldiers out in the field as a coffee substitute, although a bitter one. To make beads from these seeds, drill them lengthwise, beginning at the seed's scar (the hilum) where it was attached to the bean pod. Harvest the seeds from September or October into early spring. (See the projects on pages 87 and 114.)

Magnolia (*Magnolia* spp.) is found in many species that are native to North America. These trees produce interesting and attractive seed pods in the summer, each filled with brilliant red seeds. The seeds do not make good beads, as they shrivel and are a little soft. But the stem of the seed pod has an interesting texture that makes great beads. I cut out the textured section with a fine-tooth saw and then drill a hole lengthwise through it. Harvest magnolia pods beginning in late summer and into early fall. (See the photo on page 29.)

Mescal Bean (*Sophora secundiflora*), also known as Texas mountain laurel, is a small, slow-growing tree that's native to West Texas and New Mexico. In spring, the tree produces grape-smelling purple flowers similar to Chinese wisteria blooms. Following the flowers come velvety green or gray seed pods, each 2 to 4 inches (5-10 cm) long and containing one or more bright red, robust

seeds. In the past, these seeds were used in a Red Bean Dance by Native Americans of New Mexico for their hallucinogenic effects. Since the seeds are also highly toxic if ingested in varying doses, they were replaced in rituals by mescaline derived from the peyote cactus, as a safer source of psychotropic substances. The seed is also known commonly as coral bean. Take care not to confuse mescal beans with a different plant known as coral bean (*Erythrina herbacea*). Because this seed is toxic, do not keep it around children or pets. Harvest them from fall to spring. (See the projects on pages 49 and 66.)

Moonflower (*Calonyction aculeatum*) will provide you with fragrant summer nights in your garden. *Calonyction* means beautiful night. Plant so the vine will climb a trellis or other support. Allow its seeds to mature on the vine, and then harvest them for use as beads. The seeds are angular—they usually have three faces—and are creamy white to almost red in color as they age. They are difficult to transplant, so plant the seeds where they are to remain. (See the projects on page 52.)

Palmetto (*Sabal palmetto*, cabbage palm; *Sabal minor*, dwarf palmetto; *Serenoa repens*, saw palmetto) is one of the few native North American palms; most other familiar palm varieties were introduced to this country from tropical habitats. You can harvest the fruits and seeds from late autumn to winter. Palmetto seeds are very compact and hard. They are also prone to weevil infestation. Since the weevil often lays its eggs in the flower's ovary before the seed has been formed, you may not see signs of impending infestation. Make sure you freeze palmetto seeds for at least three days before you use them. When you drill holes in them, don't allow the drill bit to overheat in the seed's endosperm, since it heats up quickly, much like plastic. (See the projects on pages 46, 48, and 52.)

Pawpaw (*Asimina triloba*) is a small shrub or tree that bears banana-shaped fruit, each about 4 to 5 inches (10-12.5 cm) long, that contain soft yellow pulp. Handling the fruit may cause a skin rash, and, while the pulp is edible, it may cause an upset stomach in some people. Inside of each pawpaw fruit are several large, brown seeds. The seeds are a pleasant medium brown and can be drilled from end to end for necklaces and bracelets. Harvest pawpaw fruit in the fall. (See the project on page 109.)

Common Persimmon (*Diospyros virginiana*), which grows wild in North America, produces an edible fruit slightly smaller than that of the persimmon found in grocery stores. Native persimmon fruits have brown, flat, slightly iridescent seeds that are easy to gather and easy to work with. You can harvest the ripe fruit from September to November. Since per-

simmon fruit can stay a long time on the tree before deteriorating or falling off, you can find them well after their season; I've been able to harvest black and shriveled fruits as late as March.

Soapberry (*Sapindus drummondii*, western soapberry; *Sapindus saponaria*, wingleaf soapberry) trees produce clusters of yellow-orange, translucent fruits in the fall that you can harvest from September to late winter. The gummy skin and flesh of these fruits contain a substance that produces a lather in water, hence its name. This same substance is toxic and can be irritating, so make sure you wash your hands thoroughly after handling the fruits. Each fruit contains a hard, black seed, which can be used as is or polished in a rock tumbler. Drill the seeds lengthwise with a sharp drill bit. (See the project on page 104.)

SPICE ROUTES

Spices were once more valuable than gold for their use in flavoring and preserving food. Because of the scarcity of their natural habitats, spices were a prized commodity that have been a source of trade and conflict. Cinnamon, for instance, was brought to Europe by the Portuguese, who invaded Sri Lanka (formerly Ceylon) in the 17th Century to obtain supplies. In another example, Portuguese traders dominated the trade in nutmeg and mace until the Dutch took power of Indonesia in 1602. And clove trees in the Molucca Islands of Indonesia were burned by the controlling Dutch in the early 1800s to raise the price of the cloves.

Today, you can do your hunting and gathering for spices in grocery stores and in markets that specialize in international foods. Unusual spices may be obtained from botanical suppliers. Purchase some of the more fragile spices, like star anise in bulk, giving you a chance to pick out unbroken "flowers." When you are not wearing the jewelry you make, you can preserve the aroma of the spices by storing your creations in sealable plastic bags.

Allspice (*Pimenta dioca*) is the dried, unripe berries of the allspice tree that thrives in tropical climates. Allspice trees grow wild in Jamaica. Drill these round berries starting at the stem end of the seed, where there is a small indentation. (See the projects on pages 88 and 90.)

Cinnamon (*Cinnamomum zeylanicum*) is the bark of the trees of the Cinnamomum genus. To prepare, break rolls of curled cinnamon bark into small pieces, approximately ½ to 1 inch (1.5-2.5 cm) long, and drill them crosswise for stringing. (See the project on page 88.)

Cloves (*Syzygium aromaticum*), whole and dried as we know them, are actually the unopened flower buds of the clove plant. It's said that in Imperial China, one had to sweeten one's breath with cloves before approaching the emperor. To prepare, drill holes crosswise through the stem with a very small drill bit (#70 or smaller). Though tedious work, it will pay off in wonderfully fragrant necklaces. (See the project on page 88.)

Nutmeg (*Myristica fragrans*) comes from the endosperm (the seed material) of the fruit of this tropical tree. When the fruit appears on the tree, it looks like a smooth hickory nut. Inside the fruit is the nutmeg seed encased in a lacy, red material. This plant part is called an "aril"; we know it as the spice mace. With age, the red mace becomes brittle, and its color changes to peach or tan. Whole nutmeg can easily be sliced with a small, fine-tooth saw, or the whole seeds can be drilled and strung. Nutmeg used in small amounts as a spice is safe to consume; in large quantities it is toxic. (See the project on page 90.)

Star Anise (*Illicium verum*) flowers are star-shaped seed pods of a small evergreen tree native to China. The seeds have a delightful licorice-like taste and fragrance; the pods make wonderful central pendants for aromatic necklaces. Star anise may be difficult to find at your local grocery store. Try looking for it at markets

that carry international foods and spices, or order it from botanical suppliers. The pods are fairly fragile, so handle and store them carefully. They are best used in jewelry with soft wire wrapped around the "petals." (See the project on page 88.)

Seeds

Seeds (called "disseminules" in the field of botany) are the means by which plants reproduce, or propagate. Most seed-bearing plants fall into one of two categories: gymnosperms (exposed seeds), and angiosperms (seeds enclosed in a pod or ovary). Most of the seeds in this book come from angiosperms, whose seeds are generally categorized in one of two categories: the monocots and the dicots.

Monocots have one piece of endosperm which is the seeds food source for the first few weeks of its new life. Monocots produce one shoot when they germinate instead of two separate leaves. An acorn, for example, is a monocot, for it has one piece of endosperm (the "meat" of the acorn) and produces a single stem when it first breaks ground.

Dicots have an endosperm which is separated into two parts and produces a stem with two seed leaves attached to it when it germinates. These two seed leaves are the original two sections of the ungerminated endosperm. Each of these two seed leaves are cotyledons, or the first leaves to emerge. Beans, for example, are dicots

Flotsam and Jetsam

Flotsam, in maritime legal terms, is floating debris from a wrecked or sunken ship; jetsam is whatever has been jettisoned from a sinking vessel to lighten the load. However, I've always used the two terms together to include all the weird and strange objects that show up on the beach with the shifting winds and changing tides, including seashells, drift seeds, wood, cork floats, rope, and even scientific instruments.

Since the seashore seems to be my natural habitat, it's where I find most of my jewelry-making materials. People often ask how I find things on the beach when they see nothing worth picking up. Successful beachcombing is a skill that's enjoyable to learn and to practice—all it takes is the persistence to spend time looking carefully at every object at your feet.

Before you go to the seashore, browse through field guides and books with pictures of things you think you might find. You don't need to cover vast distances. Over the years, most of my extravagant beach-stuff collection has come from the same one-mile (1.6 km) stretch.

A Few Words About Environmental Issues

Make sure you know the local laws of the seashore which you can find through your state's parks and wildlife department. The best rule to follow, regardless of location, is to avoid taking a live animal from its seashell in order to collect the shell—there's an infinite number of uninhabited seashells on the beach for collecting.

Always check shells for hermit crabs, which have no shells of their own—they live in borrowed real estate. Hermit crabs can be fatally injured from the trauma of being pulled out of their shell. And, with inadequate protection from predators, they'll be quickly absorbed into the food chain. (To learn how to safely evict a hermit crab, see page 36.)

When you purchase seashells in a shop, be aware that some dealers sell shells that have been caught with live animals in them. The animals are then killed, and the shells emptied. While these shells are very good specimens—shiny and unbroken—they lack the character of those you collect yourself that have been washed up on the beach and are uninhabited by live animals.

Bone as material for jewelry and trinkets, is known as "poor man's ivory," for, when polished, it looks enough like ivory to fool the casual observer. All kinds of bones show up on the beach: fish bones, cow bones, and unidentifiable small bits of bone. Bone that has been aged by sun, sand, or water is white; newer bone ranges from gray to yellow.

All bone, whether old or new, needs to be cleaned and disinfected before you work with it. To clean fresh bone, scrub off all meat and other matter, boil it in water for a few hours, let it cool, then soak it for a day or two in a strong solution of three parts hydrogen peroxide to one part water. Next, place the bone outside to dry and bleach naturally in the sun. When you're certain the bone is clean, you can then make beads, disks, or pendants from it.

To make a flat piece, or disk, you'll need to collect a large bone with a wide surface area. To make a 2-inch (5-cm) flat square, for instance, you'll need a big bone—perhaps a cow thigh bone. If the bone is thick enough, you can shave it down until you have a flat piece.

To make beads from bone, collect long hollow bones, such as chicken legs and wing bones, then clean and disinfect them. Place them in a vise to hold them securely, then use a fine-tooth craft saw or a rotary saw blade on a craft drill to make slices as thin or thick as you desire. Note that bone produces an unpleasant odor when you cut or drill it at high speeds, especially if your tool heats up. If the odor bothers you, or if you think you may be inhaling bone dust, wear a dust mask as you work.

Polish bone by buffing it with progressively finer abrasive material. If the bone is coarse, start with coarse sandpaper (#100) then work your way up to #400 or #600. When you're finished sanding, polish or buff the bone with a soft cloth, or a buffing wheel attachment for a craft drill. If the bone is relatively fine-grained, you will need no further processing to achieve a nice finish. If the bone is coarse and porous, apply a good furniture wax to give it a smoother finish. (See the projects on pages 49, 54, 62, 64, and 70.)

Drift Seeds— A Beachcomber's Delight

Drift seeds are plant seeds that fall into the world's oceans and wash up on beaches far from their origins. Some drift seeds may have traveled via inland rivers down to the shore; others may have fallen into rivers thousands of miles away and landed on the beach days or even years after they fell from their parent plant. They float by means of either lighter-than-water material that makes up the seed coat and endosperm (the material inside), or by means of one or more air pockets inside the seed, often between two halves of the endosperm.

Some seeds that land on foreign beaches germinate, grow, and become naturalized residents. The coconut palm, found throughout the world's tropical zones, is actually native only to Indochina. The rest of the world's coconut palms were dispersed around the world by sea travel or in the hands of travelers.

You can find drift seeds on ocean beaches all over the world. Before you go out, familiarize yourself with pictures or photographs of drift seeds, so that you'll know what you're looking for. The best time to comb the beach for them is after a storm, when the wind and water currents bring in flotsam and jetsam from afar. The more matter on the beach—driftwood, seaweed, and shells—the better your chance of finding seeds, for they are often caught in floating rafts of seaweed or other drifting materials which eventually come ashore.

Always look for seeds at the highest tide line, which may be up to or in dunes on sandy beaches. And remember to look carefully, for seeds may be camouflaged with barnacles, algae, and other encrustations. Following are a few drift seeds that make wonderful jewelry.

Nickernuts (*Caesalpinia bonduc*) grow on tropical shrubs and are carried by rivers and ocean currents. The seeds, which are smooth and gray with a porcelain-like crackle finish, make great jewelry. Also called nicker beans and sea pearls, they are used in a game played in several tropical regions. This game is known as Wauri in West Africa and as Mancala in Asia and Africa.

Nickernuts are easy to grow; the seeds germinate easily, but the plant needs a very long, sunny, and warm growing season to produce seed. The plant is a sprawling shrub with hostile, prickly stickers—grow them under your windows and you'll never fear of burglars. Not all nickernuts that drift onto the beach will grow; some have been at sea too long. When you find them, collect as many as you can, so that you will have several to plant.

Wauri game from Africa with nickernuts

A quick buffing of the seed with a soft cloth produces a nice shine—and a nice static shock in winter. Children who live in areas where these plants grow have fun rubbing the seeds until they're hot, then touching someone's skin with them. (See the project on page 96.)

Prickly Palm (*Acrocomia* spp.) seeds are not very attractive when they wash up on the beach—the ones I find are mottled gray and lumpy. However, when polished in a rock tumbler, they become hard, shiny, and sturdy beads with a characteristic star-shaped scar on the bottom. They're relatively large, ½ to 1¼ inches (1.5-3 cm) in diameter, and nearly round, making them an excellent central bead for a necklace. Drill seeds with a sharp bit. (See the project on page 66.)

Sea Bean (*Mucuna urens*) is also known as hamburger bean, ox-eye, and horse eye. It comes from the bean pods of a tropical rain forest vine. The sea beans I find on the Gulf Coast of the United States probably come from the Caribbean and Central and South America. Sea beans are naturally attractive, with their brown "faces" and shiny black band

around the seed's circumference. They take a mirror finish if polished by hand or in a rock tumbler. Drill them through the black bands, either through their front or sideways. (See the project on page 96.)

Sea Heart (*Entada gigas*), also known as monkey ladder and Columbus bean (*fava de Colom* in Portugal), is one of the loveliest seeds that washes up on world shores. These seeds fall into sea-bound waterways in tropical rain forests and are carried by ocean currents to shores as far away as Norway. Christopher Columbus found sea hearts washed up on beaches of the Azores near Portugal; it is said that he was inspired by the sea heart to look for lands to the west.

Its fast-growing, climbing vine (*liana*), found in the rain forests of Central and South America, produces the longest bean pod in the world, reaching up to 6 feet (1.8 m) in length, and comprised of 15 or more compartments, each containing one seed. The seeds are woody, rich chocolate-brown in color, and large—some up to 3 inches (7.5 cm) wide.

A similar seed is the snuffbox bean (*Entada phaseoloides*), which grows throughout Old World tropics and looks like a sea heart that's been compressed into a rectangle. Before the advent of plastics, they were hollowed out and used as small boxes for holding snuff.

Sea hearts and snuffbox beans are fun to work with, since they are ready-made boxes. They can be sliced to make a compact or locket, stippled with brass wire, or left plain.

You can polish a sea heart by hand or in a rock tumbler. With persistence and patience, you can achieve a mirror finish. To polish by hand, sand with a coarse-grit sandpaper (#100) until you've removed the textured surface. Then sand with progressively finer grits (#400 then #600). When the seed is as smooth as desired, polish it with jeweler's rouge on a cloth, or use jeweler's rouge on a buffing wheel for a craft drill.

To polish a sea heart in a rock tumbler, start with coarse, dry grit (#60). You may be tempted to use water since the seeds are so sturdy, but the moisture and constant abrasion may cause them to spring leaks, then pucker. If the seed is encrusted with barnacles or other matter, tumble with #60 grit for one week. Otherwise, tumble with medium grit (#100-#200) for up to four weeks, then with a fine grit (#400-#600) for approximately two weeks. After tumbling, polish the seed by hand using a jeweler's cloth, or polish with jeweler's rouge on a buffing wheel attachment for a craft drill. You can also continue to tumble the seed for one to two weeks using the polishing agent, rouge-coated crushed walnut shells. (See the projects on pages 56, 58, and 121.)

Glass that is found in broken abundance on city streets and parking lots, beaches, parks, and in many other wildlife habitats is not a natural material. Fortunately, you can change these colorful shards from trash to treasure and clean a little bit of the environment at the same time.

I've included glass in this section because many of you have collected bits of beach glass—those smooth frosted, opaque pieces of blue, amber, green, or white that have been tempered by sea and sand. Many bits of beach glass that you find are almost ready-made pieces of jewelry, needing only a hole for stringing, or wire for wrapping.

For glass found in other environments, break up large pieces by placing them in a paper bag and striking with a hammer until you have the size pieces you want. Then tumble them in a rock tumbler for 24 hours with coarse (#60-#100) silicon-carbide grit. The tumbling process will smooth sharp edges and frost the glass. To drill holes in the tumbled pieces, use a craft drill with a diamond-coated bit following the instructions for drilling hard materials found on page 24. (See the projects on pages 54 and 70.)

Seashells fall in several categories but the two most common are gastropods and bivalves. Gastropods are snails; bivalves are clams—and there are many more gastropods than bivalves.

One of my favorite shells, the lightning whelk, is an unusual gastropod, in that it spirals to the left instead of to the right, as do most other gastropods. This seashell can be found on Atlantic and Gulf Coasts of the United States, and can grow to 18 inches (45.5 cm) long. Females bear intriguing strings of egg cases. The strings can be up to 36 inches (91.5 cm) long, containing dozens of leathery capsules. Each capsule can contain up to 100 baby whelks, complete with tiny seashells. At the right time, a hole forms in each capsule and the babies crawl out into the world. Like all clams and snails, whelks secrete liquid calcium carbonate that hardens to form their shell. Other whelks, right-handed ones, are found on world shores. (See the projects on pages 62, 68, 82, and 100.)

Shark Teeth are arranged row after row in the shark's mouth; as old teeth are shed or lost, new ones take their place. When beachcombing, you'll need time, patience, and practice to see and find them, for they're easily missed among other shells. I've had the best luck when the tide is low and large collections of small shells lie in piles, or windrows, leading into the surf. Try to collect as many teeth as you can, so that you will be able to match sizes for earrings.

Fossilized shark teeth are found inland in the United States at the sites of ancient seas. They are also found washed up on beaches. To accurately determine whether a beached shark tooth is a fossil, you'll need the advice of a paleontologist.

Shark teeth are versatile as a jewelry material. You can wind them tightly with wire to make a pendant or earrings. Or, you can drill holes in them with a hobby drill, using a sharp, diamond-coated bit (see page 24), so you can hang them from a cord or chain. (See the project on page 84).

HOW TO EVICT A HERMIT CRAB

If you want to collect a shell inhabited by a hermit crab, never pull the crab out of its home. It is better to persuade the crab to move into a different shell.

To do this, first place the hermit crab in a tide pool or bucket of seawater. Then, place an empty shell, about the same size or larger than the crab's present shell, a few inches (cm) from the hermit crab. Wait a few minutes and watch.

If in the mood, the crab will approach the empty shell, take a look at it, then walk around it. It may turn it upside down, emptying any sand or debris in the shell, then measure the opening for fit with its claws. If the crab is still interested, it will move its shell up to the new one, until there's very little space between the two. Then it will grab the opening of the new shell with its claws, and go frontwards into it to look it over.

If it likes what it sees, the crab will back out, grab the opening with his claws, and vault back end first into the new shell. At this point, leave the crab alone for awhile, since it may move back and forth from shell to shell until it's satisfied. Once its made its decision—hopefully for the new shell—collect the old shell before the crab decides to switch back again.

Distant Lands

In roaming my suburban neighborhood for jewelry materials, I quickly found that many trees and shrubs hail from almost everywhere except North America. Even plants found in vacant lots which appear to flourish as native growth actually have their origins on the other side of the world.

Because I live in a subtropical region of the United States, my area is heavily cultivated with ornamental plants from similar climates from around the world. Lawns are trimmed in the spring with azalea blooms of red, white, peach, and lavender—all from Japan. The South, Georgia and South Carolina in particular, is carpeted from lawn to forest canopy with the pernicious plant kudzu, also imported from Japan.

Many areas of North America can nurture the beautiful and fragrant blossoms of white and lavender wisteria from China.

One of my favorite materials to use is seed pods of eucalyptus trees from Australia. Many varieties have been introduced to California and other warm regions of the United States and yield unique flowers and great woody pods that make dramatic personal ornaments.

Investigate your area for non-native plants or visit plant nurseries for some of the materials to use or seeds for growing your own. If you plan on raising your own plants, make sure that the introduced (non-native) plant is still a welcomed one. Some vegetation, especially kudzu, which was introduced for cultivation as cattle feed, has outgrown its usefulness and has nearly submerged the southern United States in green.

African Porcupine Quills
(*Hystricidas family*) are lethal-looking quills that come from a porcupine that lives in Africa. They can be purchased from several suppliers and make show-stopping hair sticks and elegant beads. Have fun making hair sticks by attaching attractive objects to the quills using a loop of wire, chain, or thread. For quick beads, simply cut the quills crosswise. Just make sure you file or sand off the sharp ends before you work with them. (See the projects on pages 76 and 100.)

(See the projects on pages 76 and 100.)

Start Your Own Herbarium

A collection of properly stored specimens with their leaves, fruits, flowers, and any other representative parts, such as twigs, thorns, bark, seeds, and seed pods, is called an herbarium. To start your own, begin by keeping a record of the vital statistics of each specimen you collect. Include when and where you found it (noting latitude and longitude, the city, state, and country), by whom (including whomever was with you), and under what weather conditions.

Be sure to record the size and shape of the plant, whether or not the plant has a fragrance, thorns, and if it weeps sticky fluid when bruised or cut. These are some of the criteria used by botanists to identify both old and new species. It's also wise to take photographs of the specimens that are in your herbarium before drying and storing them, for the plants' colors can fade or change as they dry.

You can take a plant press or old phone books out in the field with you so you can press the plant parts as soon as you collect them. Clean and dry the specimens well before placing them in the book or press, since wet specimens may mildew or rot. Press all plant parts until they are dry and flat. Professional herbaria keep specimens that have been sewn or glued to high-quality, acid-free rag bond paper. Many art and photography supply stores carry archival paper suitable for keeping specimens.

Bamboo (*Phyllostachys* spp.), a grass native to Asia, is one of the most useful plants in the world—houses are built of it, its shoots are eaten, its leaves are used for painting, and its culms (stalks) are cut, bent, split, and polished to make an almost endless variety of decorative and functional objects. The cylindrical structure of bamboo makes it quite strong and provides a vertical grain that is easy to split. You can split pieces by hand if they are small in diameter. To split larger pieces, use a sharp knife to start the split at the top of the bamboo section, then either continue using the knife, or remove the knife and split by hand.

You can bend bamboo by heating it over a flame (an oil lamp works best). To do this, use strips that are ¼ inch (.5 cm) wide or less, heating small 1-inch (2.5-cm) lengths of the piece at a time. Make sure you hold the bamboo high enough above the flame so it doesn't char. Heat the section until the waxy coat on the outer surface begins to melt and the bamboo begins to soften. When the section is pliable, bend it until you've achieved the desired curve. Move on to the next section and repeat. If you're bending a short section of bamboo, hold the ends with pliers so that you don't burn your fingers. You can sand the ends of bamboo to make them even and

smooth, and polish and buff the outer surface, using the natural wax for shine. See pags17-18 for information on growing bamboo. (See the projects on pages 66, 76, and 120.)

Chinaberry Trees

(*Melia azedarach*), also called bead trees, come from China. Their beige, ribbed seeds have been used for eons for prayer beads, rosaries, and necklaces. The tree is fairly easy to identify even in winter, since the yellow fruits, which look like tiny apples hanging in clusters from the branches, stay on the tree long after they've ripened. The fruits are foul smelling, making them unpleasant to work with, but the seeds are well worth the effort of collecting and cleaning them.

To make beads, soak the fruits in warm water for a few days until they are soft and can be easily removed. Put the soggy fruits in a colander under running water, then use your hands to rub the skin and flesh off each seed. Though the separated seeds may seem a bit slimy and fleshy at first, they'll turn out nicely once dried in the sun or food dehydrator. They have a fibrous coating that you can leave on or remove by putting them in a rock tumbler for a few days with coarse grit and water. The seeds are easily dyed (follow the instructions for dyeing melon and squash seeds on page 44), and if desired, you

can polish them after removing their "fuzz" in a rock tumbler.

Though chinaberry seeds naturally have a hole in one end, it often doesn't go through to the other side, so you will have to do a little drilling to make proper beads. Drill the seeds from the flatter end, where the fruit was attached to its stem. Be aware that the flesh of the seeds is toxic. (See the projects on page 72.)

Chinese Wisteria (*Wisteria chinensis*) plants are perennial woody vines or shrubs that produce strong and heavy limbs. If not controlled, they can destroy structures. Grown on a strong support or as a bush, these deciduous plants produce abundant and fragrant purple flowers in the spring. In the summer, velvety green pods appear. Each pod has several flat brown seeds, which have wavelike concentric ridges. The pods are interesting in that they pop open and propel their seeds. (A pod, left on my work table for several days, popped open with a bang and sent seeds ricocheting off the walls.) The seeds are flat and thin. You can drill them through their flat faces, or drill a hole near the top of each seed to make beads that can be hung from a thread or attached to a chain or wire with a jump ring. Since wisteria seeds are inviting food for insects, disinfect them in the freezer for three days, then store them in an airtight, bug-proof container. See page 18 for information on growing wisteria. (See the project on page 61.)

Coconut Palms (*Cocos nucifera*) are one of the most valuable of all food and economic plants. Their huge seeds are the source of oil used in soaps and cosmetics, in cooking, and as an industrial lubricant. The fibrous husks are used for rope and cordage, for garden mulch, and as a potting soil substitute. The endosperm is the white coconut meat you use in cooking. You can readily find coconuts in any grocery store. Like many members of the enormous palm family, the shell of the seed is very hard. You can cut it open using a sharp machete, a hacksaw, a radial arm saw, or by bashing it with a hammer. You can also break the shell by dropping it on a hard outdoor surface, such as a patio or driveway. This tough shell makes wonderful jewelry material. You can cut the shell into any shape and can polish the surface to a mirror finish using progressively finer grades of sandpaper or sanding drums on a craft drill. If you enjoy the coconut's flavor, purchase green coconuts in their husk and drink the liquid inside. (See the projects on pages 54, 64, 78, 83, and 100.)

Eucalyptus (*Eucalyptus* spp.) originates in Australia, which is home to a great number of varieties, some of which have come to North America. You may be most familiar with the eucalyptus that produces the flat, round, aromatic leaves found in craft supply stores and at florist shops. However, it's the blue gum (*Eucalyptus globulus*) and red gum (*Eucalyptus ficifolia*) that produce the woody seed pods that make excellent jewelry material. If you have these trees in your area, you can collect your own pods or you can also order them from a commercial supplier. I often purchase a mix of dried plant material for use in flower arrangements and wreaths that contain eucalyptus seed pods and other foreign fruits and nuts. Working with eucalyptus pods provides an added treat—a wonderful fragrance wafts up as you drill your holes. (See the project on pages 92).

Gingko Tree (*Gingko biloba*), also called maidenhair fern and maidenhair tree, has left records of its prehistoric past in fossils that have been found in locations far from its native country of China. Recent research has revealed memory-enhancing properties of this plant which have brought gingko biloba to the market place. Gingko trees have been introduced to the United States and grow under almost any condition. To identify the tree, look for its distinctive, fan-shaped leaves that grow right off the main branches. Each tree is either male or female, with more males planted than females because of the repulsive aroma of the female fruit. If you collect the fruits, soak them in water, remove the flesh and meat, and dry the beige seeds. Drill the seeds lengthwise to make interesting beads. You can also crack open the seed to find a green kernel, which may be roasted and eaten. The kernel is featured in a Japanese custardlike soup called *chawan-mushi*. (See the projects on pages 87 and 114.)

Job's Tears (*Coix lacryma-jobi*) are the true gems of the botanical bead world, for they are the most widely and commonly used botanical bead material. Mother Theresa of Calcutta was buried with her rosary made of Job's tears. The plant is a member of the same family (*Graminae*) as corn and maize. It's easy to grow, but you'll need ample vertical space, since the stalks can be 10 feet (3 m) tall. The seeds, which the plant produces prolifically, aren't actually seeds; they're tear-shaped involucres (bracts) that enclose female flowers. The seeds require no preparation before using in jewelry. You don't even need to drill them; merely pierce them with needle and thread, a head pin, or a piece of wire. See page 19 for information on growing Job's tears. (See the project on page 94.)

Lotus

(*Nelumbo nuciferum*, *Nelumbo lutea*), revered in the Buddhist faith, is a plant cultivated in many cultures for its beauty and its culinary contributions. Just about every part is edible: the root, often sold in Asian markets, is served sliced, revealing a beautiful pattern of holes; and the seeds can be collected and eaten either immature and green or after being roasted. The seed pods, sold in craft stores and nurseries, are attractive by themselves or in dried flower arrangements. Look for lotus plants in wet, swampy areas, such as in small lakes and ponds and in roadside ditches, frequently close to stands of cattails. The seeds, when mature, are a dull chocolate brown and are easily pierced with a hand or power drill for use as beads. The seeds can be left as is, or can be polished by hand or with buffing wheels on a craft drill. See page 19 for information on growing lotus.

Soy Bean (See page 44.)

Rain Forest and Tropics

The rain forests and equatorial regions of the earth are home to some of the world's most intriguing plants. Many of these have been cultivated by native peoples to provide raw materials to other countries for making a variety of useful items. One of these plants is a South American palm tree that was cultivated in Ecuador. Its seed, the tagua nut, provided raw material to the button trade in the United States before plastics overwhelmed the market. You can see examples of tagua nut buttons, carvings, and jewelry on pages 10 and 11. Another plant once used for commerce is the candlenut tree of the South Pacific, whose seeds provided fuel for torches and soot for tattoo ink.

If you have an opportunity to visit tropical areas, you may not be able to bring seeds or vegetation into your own country due to customs regulations. However, you can purchase these seeds from a seed supplier or plant nursery that specializes in tropical plants. Just make sure that the materials you acquire are grown and harvested in an environmentally responsible way.

At this writing, there are many environmental groups working with rain forest populations to best utilize their raw materials and labor. Check your library or other reference sources for current groups and organizations who can provide you with specific information about obtaining these materials without causing ecological harm.

Mary's Bean, of all the seeds that fall into the ocean, travels the farthest and may drift about for months or  years. It has been known to drift all the way to Norway from the rain forests of Mexico and Central America. This vine has rarely been seen growing in the wild. The plant, *Merremia discoidesperma*, is named after the Virgin Mary. On one side of the seed, indentations create a cross pattern that is likened to the Christian crucifix. Because of the distance they travel, Mary's beans are said to bring safety and good luck to travelers on water. It is also believed that a mother will have an easier childbirth when holding the seed (See the project on page 94.)

Bauhinia (*Bauhinia variegata* and other species) is also called orchid tree. The flat, black seeds are perfect when you need a black accent. Drill and string them through their faces, the widest part of the seed. (See Hawaiian seed lei on page 8.)

Candlenut (*Aleurites moluccana*), also called kukui nut, is from the South Seas. Torches are made from the tree's oil-rich seed kernels by impaling fresh kernels on a stick and lighting them, giving the seeds their name. By charring the seed kernel, South Pacific Islanders make a dark blue dye from the soot that serves as a permanent ink for tattoos. The seeds are unremarkable in their raw state but make beautiful beads when polished. The inside, the kernel, can be left in or removed through the drill holes. You can achieve various finishes through different sanding and polishing techniques. The photo on page 8 shows a string of dark candlenuts from Hawaii. (See the project on page 100.)

Canna (*Canna* spp.) is a large genus of many varieties of what is commonly called canna lilies. The floppy flowers are usually red, orange, or yellow. Some varieties produce round seed pods containing smooth black seeds that are uniform in size, making them perfect for use as beads. One variety, indian shot (*Canna indica*), produces seeds used frequently in botanical jewelry. Canna leaves can also be used to make leaf packages (see page 119). Cannas are easy to grow and bring to seed. In warm climates, they can be grown as perennials (see page 18). Not all cannas produce seeds that can be used as beads. Before growing your own, visit or contact a nursery to familiarize yourself with available varieties that will produce suitable seeds. (See the project on page 98.)

Carob (*Ceratonia siliqua*), from which faux chocolate is made, is a tree native to the eastern Mediterranean. It was introduced to the United States in 1854 and grows in southern Florida, the Gulf states, New Mexico, Arizona, and southern California. Carob is also called St. John's bread after the legend that the pods were the "locusts" that John the Baptist ate while in the desert. For use in jewelry, drill the flat, soft-brown seeds through their "faces" to make beads.

Cycad (*Cycas revoluta*) is an ancient plant that is often mistaken for a palm tree, especially since it is also called sago palm. Cycads plants are either male or female, with the female plants producing an abundance of orange fruits. Cycad seeds germinate easily and produce an excellent house plant. If you collect your own seeds, scrape off the flesh with a paring or craft knife. If you collect seeds to use later, freeze them until you are ready to use them. (See the project on page 114.)

Elephant Ear Tree (*Enterolobium cyclocarpus*), also known as guanacaste, has a common name that refers to its large ear-shaped seed pods, which contain beautiful, tricolored seeds. They make striking beads. Polish and buff the seeds to a nice sheen in a rock tumbler by tumbling them dry with medium (#200) silicon-carbide grit for four weeks, then with rouge-coated crushed walnut shells (a polishing compound) for two weeks, or until the seeds are shiny. You can also polish and buff by hand with a jeweler's cloth. To drill, use a small, sharp bit, always starting at the flatter of the seed's two ends. (See the projects on pages 74 and 96.)

Jumbie Beads (*Adenanthera pavonia*) are seeds from the red sandlewood tree. These rich red seeds are so uniform in shape and weight that they have been used in the past to weigh gold. They are excellent as bead material and are well known as a jewelry bead in tropical areas.

Lucky Nut (*Thevetia peruviana*), also called yellow oleander, is a small evergreen tree native to tropical South America. In the West Indies, the seed is thought to bring luck and is kept or carried as a talisman. The large triangular seeds make interesting accent pieces. Try growing this plant for its shiny leaves and yellow flowers in a warm area of your garden or in pots as patio or house plants. As they are uncommon, you may need to purchase seeds or plants. NOTE: This plant and its seeds are poisonous. (See the project on page 100.)

Pindo Palm (*Butia capitata*) is a feather palm with distinctive gray-green fronds and a sweet, round, yellow fruit from which jelly can be made without the addition of pectin, hence its other common name, jelly palm. The seeds look like miniature coconuts; they are brown, very hard, have a fibrous outer coat, and three germination pores. To remove the fiber and polish the seeds, tumble them in a rock tumbler, first with coarse grit (#60-#100) for a few days, and then with progressively finer grits (#400-#600) for two weeks. You can add water to the grit in the tumbler because the seeds are so woody they will not degrade. Tumble the seeds until they have a matte finish, then polish them by tumbling them for two weeks in rouge-coated crushed walnut shells. To drill, use a sharp drill bit. Fresh seeds contain oil that smells like coconut; rub it on the seed for added sheen. (See the projects on pages 66 and 80.)

Pride of Barbados (*Delonix regia*), also called flame of the forest, royal poinciana, or flamboyant, is a tree from the tropics that produces remarkably long, woody seed pods, each with a long row of oval seeds. The attractive seed is two-toned brown and light brown. You can drill them several different ways: drill small holes on the flat face at each end of the

oval seed and string them together face-to-face; drill one hole in the flat side of one end and hang them on a necklace chain; or drill them end to end, through the center. You may need to practice to get the holes straight. (See the project on page 58.)

Tamarind (*Tamarindus indica*) trees have shiny brown seeds that are surrounded in their bean-like pods by a tart brown

FROM THE SUPERMARKET

Hunting and gathering in the supermarket is great fun. I love snooping in the aisles to find unusual foods to serve as raw materials for jewelry.

I like to go to one of the many international grocery stores that have sprung up in my city, where I find foods from India, Vietnam, China, Japan, and the West Indies. In addition to the spices commonly found in the supermarket chains, such as cinnamon, nutmeg, and pepper, I'm now

pulp. When sweetened with sugar or honey, the pulp is used to make confections and drinks. You can purchase the pods and seeds in grocery stores that carry tropical foods. For jewelry, remove the seeds from the pulp, wash them off, then dry them on paper towels or in a food dehydrator. They have a natural polish and can be drilled through the flat faces or from end to end. (See the project on page 102.)

able to find a wonderful variety of mysterious spices. One of my favorites is copal (*Elaphrium jorullense*) from Mexico, amber-colored chunks of resin. When you melt some of the chunks in hot water, you can mold them into round beads that look like marbled plastic.

Stores that carry international foods also yield melons with interesting seeds, lots of different kinds of beans, canned peach palm fruits with palm seeds still in them, whole nutmeg, star anise, and many spices I've never heard of and haven't quite figured out how to use. In the produce section, look for **tamarind beans** with the seeds inside them (see page 42), fresh coconuts, plums, and cherries. Look also for good wrapping and decorating materials such as banana leaves, lemon grass, and fresh mint.

Don't forget to visit health food stores and stores that specialize in botanicals. You can find all kinds of interesting seeds, berries, barks, and dried flowers used in a variety of alternative healing therapies.

Apples and **Oranges** are certainly easy to find year-round, but they both have few seeds per fruit. If you have an orchard, or consume enormous amounts of these fruits, then you'll be able to adorn yourself from head to toe. Apple seeds make nice necklaces because of their color. You can make holes in apple seeds by piercing them with a sewing needle. Citrus seeds require drilling.

Beans come in an amazing variety of colors and patterns: scarlet runner beans, pinto beans, Mexican black beans, jack beans, fava beans, cowpeas, and hyacinth beans. You'll find exotic-looking dried beans in the international food sections of the supermarket or in specialty stores. One small warning: Don't get caught in a monsoon wearing dried bean jewelry; your jewelry may swell—or, perhaps, sprout! See page 18 for information on growing beans. (See the project on page 102.)

Calypso Beans are black-and-white beans that are handsome all by themselves in a necklace with small gold or silver spacer

beads and a clasp. It's easy to see why they are sometimes called yin-yang seeds. They look especially nice against saturated reds and yellows. These seeds also look nice with red seeds, such as coral beans or mescal beans. Drill holes in them lengthwise, taking care not to split apart the two halves of the bean. Since their skin is thin and may chip off with wear, it's best to seal them with a coat of clear gloss acrylic spray. (See the project on page 50.)

Cherries and **Plums** are stone fruits; that is, they have hard-shelled seeds in the center of their endosperm (the part you eat). Because their seeds are hard and tough, they make super beads. To prepare the seeds for beading, wash the pits to remove any remaining flesh from the fruit. Then scrub them with a scrub brush or old toothbrush. Spread the cleaned pits on paper towels to dry. If you want smooth beads, you can put them in a rock tumbler with coarse grit (#100) for a few days. Cherry pits don't dye well, but plum pits do.

Coconut (See page 39.)

Coffee Beans are naturally hard and well suited for use as beads. Besides, you can brew up a cup or two of coffee while you make

jewelry. Simply place some coffee beans in a colander and rinse them with cool water to remove any powdery coatings that may have been added for flavor, then spread them on a paper towel to dry. Drill holes in the beans either lengthwise or crosswise, and you have beads. If you get tired of your necklace or find yourself entirely too sleepy at the office after lunch, brew your jewelry! (See the project on page 102.)

Dried Peas have a cool, celadon-green color and a wrinkled texture. Since they are moderately hard, drill them with a hobby drill using a $\frac{1}{16}$-inch (.16 cm) bit (or smaller). They look especially good with contrasting shapes, such as the flat, thin seeds of the cantaloupe. (See the project on page 112.)

Melon and **Squash** seeds are plentiful and versatile jewelry materials. Choose melons and squashes with large seeds, such as cantaloupe, honeydew melon, watermelon, acorn squash, and butternut squash. All of these have seeds that are easy to extract—simply put them in a colander with the stringy melon parts attached. Under running water, stir them around briskly to remove the flesh, then spread them out on paper towels to dry. These seeds do not need to be drilled. You can pierce them with a sewing needle, then string them on a piece of beading thread.

Melon and squash seeds, with the exception of watermelon seeds, take dye well and can be dyed both bright and rich colors with common clothing dye, also from the grocery store. To dye the seeds, empty the dye into a pint-sized (.5 L) container with a watertight lid. Fill the container about ¾ full with warm water and stir until the dye dissolves. Drop the seeds into the dye mixture and let them soak for as long as you want—the longer you soak them, the richer the color. Generally, seeds will reach maximum dye saturation after about 12 hours. You may want to remove a few seeds periodically to check the color. Remember that dyed seeds will look darker when wet. See page 19 for information on growing melons and squash. (See the projects on pages 50, 102, and 112.)

Peaches are truly one of the divine foods of the earth. If you enjoy them, save the pits. These odd, wrinkled objects make lovely earrings and necklaces if you clean, sand, and polish the pits. Use split halves for earrings. Prepare them by scrubbing them briskly with a wire brush under running water to remove

remaining flesh. Allow them to dry thoroughly. Sand the pits starting with coarse (#200) sandpaper, and finishing with progressively finer sandpapers (#400 and #600). You can also smooth them by tumbling them in a rock tumbler with coarse grit and water, followed by medium and fine grit, but I have found that the pit absorbs the gray color of the silicon carbide and water, which is difficult to remove, as are the fine grains of grit. Once smoothed to your satisfaction, apply a clear spray varnish in either matte, semigloss, or gloss finish.

Soy Bean (*Glycine max.*) is one of the world's most important foods, especially in its ancestral homes of China, Japan, and Taiwan. The seed is rich in nutrients, being approximately 20% oil and 45 to 48% protein. This hardy annual grows up to 2 feet (60 cm) tall and has hairy seed pods, each containing one to four seeds. You can buy seeds in the grocery stores. They make excellent beads, although they're somewhat fragile. They split easily when drilled, so drill them sideways rather than through the ends. Since the seed coat is fairly thin and will deteriorate with abrasion, use these seeds in necklaces instead of in bracelets. (See the project on page 102.)

Toxic Plants and Plant Parts

If you have any doubts about plant toxicity, make sure you investigate all unfamiliar plants to see if they might be poisonous.

Apple seeds (in quantity)

Avocado—leaves, bark, seed

Holly berries

Chinese tallow seeds

Croton—foliage, shoots

Dieffenbachia (dumb cane)—all parts

Dogwood—fruit

Elderberry—foliage

Equisetum (horse tail)—all parts

Horse chestnut (buckeye)—nuts, twigs

Jasmine—foliage, flowers sap

Star Jasmine—foliage, flowers

Jimson weed (Datura stramonium)

Johnson grass—all parts

Lobelia—all parts

Locusts—all parts

Lupines

Milkweed—foliage

Mistletoe—berries

Moonseed—berries

Nickernut

Nightshades—berries, leaves

Peach pits

Pear seeds (in quantity)

Plums—foliage, inner seed

Pokeweed—roots, fruits

Soapberry

Sweet pea—seeds, fruit

Wisteria—pods and seeds

Yew—needles, seeds

PROJECTS

Acorn and Palmetto Seed Buddhist Prayer Beads

Many of the world's religions use a circle of beads as a means of holding meditative focus while praying. Each individual bead represents a prayer or mantra, allowing the supplicant to keep track of the repetitions recited. Since antiquity, natural beads have provided the materials for prayer beads. Acorns, with their smooth, woody shells, provide a way to touch the divine through the simple wonders of nature.

Materials

33 acorns

33 palmetto seeds (these are from the Sabal palm)—or, use other small, round seeds or beads

66 round gold beads, 3mm in diameter

1 yard (.9 m) of beading thread or tigertail

1 tassel (this one is an upholstery tassel)

White craft glue

Clear spray enamel or varnish (optional)

Tools

Craft drill with a 1⁄16-inch (.16-cm) drill bit, and a #61 drill bit

Scissors

Beading needle to fit the thread

Needle-nose pliers with serrated jaws

Instructions

One

Drill holes in the acorns and palmetto seeds. Use the 1⁄16-inch (.16 cm) drill bit for the acorns, and the #61 drill bit for the palmetto seeds. Drill the acorns from the top (where the cap used to be) through to the bottom. Since the palmetto seeds are small and slippery, it's best to hold them tightly in the jaws of the serrated-jaw pliers as you drill.

Two

If desired, spray the acorns and palmetto seeds with clear spray enamel or varnish. To avoid drips, it's always better to apply several light coats rather than one heavy one, allowing each coat to dry thoroughly before applying the next.

Three

Using the beading thread and beading needle, string the acorns, palmetto seeds, and gold beads as shown.

Four

When all the beads are strung, attach the tassel by threading its loop onto the beading thread.

Five

Take up any slack in the thread before tying the ends together using several strong finishing knots. For security, dot the knots with glue.

Palmetto Seed Bracelet

With their uniform shape and shiny brown finish, palmetto seeds are almost perfect natural beads.

Materials

> 21 palmetto seeds
>
> 22 round beads, 2.5mm in diameter
>
> 2 clamshell bead caps
>
> 1 piece of beading thread, approximately 12 inches (30.5 cm) long
>
> 1 jump ring, 3mm in size
>
> Lobster-claw clasp
>
> Craft glue

Tools

> Craft drill with a #61 (or ¹⁄₁₆-inch (.16 cm)) drill bit
>
> Serrated-jaw pliers
>
> Scissors
>
> Beading needle
>
> Flat-nose pliers

Instructions

One

Drill holes in the palmetto seeds. Since these seeds are small and slippery, it's best to hold them tightly in the jaws of the serrated-jaw pliers as you drill.

Two

Using approximately 12 inches (30.5 cm) of beading thread, make a knot in one end. String a bead cap onto this knotted end. Thread the free end of the thread onto the needle and string the seeds and beads, alternating gold beads and palmetto seeds. Note: To fit a specific wrist size, you may need to adjust the length of the thread and the number of seeds and beads you use.

Three

To finish, string on the second bead cap, take up any slack in the thread, and make a secure knot to fit into the bead cap. Place a dot of craft glue on the knots at both ends and allow to dry. When the glue is dry, use the flat-nose pliers to close the bead caps.

Four

Attach the jump ring to the loop end of one bead cap, then attach the lobster-claw clasp to the loop end of the other bead cap.

Bone, Palm Wood, and Mescal Bean Hoop Earrings

The elegant simplicity of these hoop earrings makes them a unique accessory for any outfit. For added interest, use a wood-burning tool to decorate the wood beads in a design of your choice.

Materials

4 small, square cow-bone beads

4 mescal beans

2 round slices of wood, approximately ½ inch (1.5 cm) in diameter and ¼ inch (.5 cm) thick (shown here, palm wood)

12 round gold beads, 3mm in diameter

2 hoop earrings, 2 inches (5 cm) in diameter

2 jump rings, 3mm in diameter

2 ear wires

Tools

Craft drill with a ¹⁄₁₆-inch (.16-cm) drill bit

Wood-burning tool

Flat-nose pliers

Instructions

ONE
Make or purchase the square bone beads. (See pages 33-34 for finding and preparing bone.)

TWO
Drill holes in the mescal beans lengthwise. Drill holes through the center of the flat sides of the wood slices and bone.

THREE
Using the wood-burning tool, decorate the wood beads in a design of your choice using zigzags, dots, and/or stripes.

FOUR
Thread the round beads, bone, wood, and mescal beans on the hoops as shown. Using the pliers, attach a jump ring and ear wire to each hoop.

Melon Seed and Calypso Bean Necklace

You can dye the melon seeds any color you want. However, this orange-red tends to work well with the black-and-white calypso beans to give this necklace a vibrant sense of movement.

Materials

28 calypso beans (dried)

145 assorted dyed melon seeds (cantaloupe, honeydew, and squash)

1 round gold bead, 5 mm in diameter

Raffia, 20 inches (51 cm)

Clear spray varnish or lacquer

Tools

Craft drill with a 1⁄16-inch (.16-cm) drill bit

Sewing or embroidery needle to fit raffia

Needle-nose pliers with serrated jaws

Scissors

Instructions

One

Follow the directions on page 44 for dyeing the melon and squash seeds. After dyeing, allow the seeds to dry thoroughly before stringing.

Two

Using the craft drill and the 1⁄16-inch (.16-cm) drill bit, drill holes lengthwise in the calypso beans.

Three

With the sewing needle and raffia, string the calypso beans and melon seeds, piercing the melon seeds with the needle as you go. For this design, there are five melon seeds between each calypso bean.

Four

To finish, tie the ends of the raffia together using a double knot. Do not trim the ends. Using both ends of raffia as one, string the gold bead onto the raffia, then make several overhand knots in the two raffia ends to secure the gold bead.

Five

Spray the entire necklace with one or two coats of spray varnish or lacquer. This will keep the seed coats of the calypso beans from coming off and the dye from the melon seeds from rubbing off on clothing. To avoid drips, it's always better to apply two light coats of varnish or lacquer than one heavy one. Always allow the first coat to dry completely before applying the second one.

Moonflower and Palmetto Seed Earrings and Necklace

Moonflower seeds, with their pale-gold color, are particularly attractive when set against gold jewelry findings. To highlight this look for these earrings and necklace, the moonflower seeds have been offset with gold beads and strung on gold dangle pins. The dark-brown palmetto seeds have been added as deeper accents to complement the overall effect.

Materials

Earrings

6 moonflower seeds

4 palmetto seeds

2 earring hoops, 32mm in diameter

10 round gold beads, 4mm in diameter

5 round gold beads, 3mm in diameter

6 jump rings, 3mm in diameter

6 gold head pins, 2 inches (5 cm) long

Necklace

14 palmetto seeds (you can substitute 14 small, round beads or seeds)

13 moonflower seeds

Gold chain with clasp, 24 inches (61 cm) long

13 dangle pins, 2 inches (5 cm) long with diamond-shaped ends

54 gold beads, 3mm in diameter

Tools

Craft drill with a ¹⁄16-inch (.16-cm) drill bit, and a #70 drill bit

Needle-nose pliers with serrated jaws

Round-nose pliers

Flat-nose pliers

Wire cutters

Instructions

Earrings

One

Using the craft drill and the ¹⁄16-inch (.16-cm) drill bit, drill holes in the moonflower seeds. Use the #70 bit to drill holes in the palmetto seeds. Start at the hilum of the seed (the flower scar on the bottom) and drill through the seed lengthwise. Drill holes in the palmetto seeds, crosswise. Since palmetto seeds are small, hard, and slippery, you may need to hold them in the needle-nose pliers with serrated jaws when drilling.

Two

To assemble each dangle, place a 4mm gold bead, followed by a moonflower seed, then a 3mm gold bead on each head pin. Make six dangles. Using the round-nose pliers, make a loop on the straight end of each head pin. With the flat-nose pliers, wrap the free end of each head pin around the pin's shaft. Trim with wire cutters if necessary.

Three

Attach a 3mm jump ring to each of these loops.

Four

On each wire ear hoop, place a 4mm gold bead, a palmetto seed, three dangles, a palmetto seed, and a 4mm gold bead. If necessary to close the hoop, use the flat-nose pliers to bend the free end of the wire hoop into a 90-degree angle, then poke this end through the hole on the other end of the hoop. (Some wire ear hoops already come this way.)

Necklace

One

Using the craft drill and the ¹⁄16-inch (.16-cm) drill bit, drill holes in the moonflower seeds. Use the #70 bit to drill holes in the palmetto seeds. Start at the hilum of the seed (the flower scar on the bottom) and drill through the seed lengthwise. Drill holes in the palmetto seeds, crosswise. Since palmetto seeds are small, hard, and slippery, you may need to hold them in the needle-nose pliers with serrated jaws when drilling.

Two

Place a gold bead, a moonflower seed, and another gold bead on the diamond-end dangle pins.

Three

With the round-nose pliers, make a loop in the free end of each dangle pin. Straighten the loops with the flat-nose pliers.

Four

Following the photograph as a guide, string the seeds, beads, and dangle pins on the 24-inch (61-cm) necklace.

Beer Bottle Glass Necklace

Horse hair makes a strong cord or beading thread. For this project, it adds a braided texture that offsets the smooth, frosted glass. If you have a horse, or know someone who does, you have a ready supply of this raw material. If not, find a supplier from the source list at the back of the book. The hair for this necklace came from an old violin bow.

Materials

7 pieces of brown beer bottle glass

11 hackberry seeds

2 flat pieces of cow bone

1 flat pebble

1 piece of coconut shell

Hank of horse hair (mixture of black, brown, and blonde), 18 inches (45.5 cm) long

Hemp twine, 15 inches (38 cm)

Craft glue

2 gold cylindrical end caps, ¼ inch (.5 cm) in diameter and ½ inch (1.5 cm) long

Epoxy glue

Black leather cord, 1 mm in diameter, approximately 6 inches (15 cm) in length

4 cord crimp ends with loops

4 jump rings, 4mm in size

Toggle and bar clasp (purchased)

Brass wire, 24-gauge

11 small, round bone beads, 3mm in diameter (purchased)

11 gold beads, 5mm in diameter

Tools

Scissors

Flat-nose pliers

Craft drill with a diamond-coated drill bit

Plastic putty

Shallow can (a cat food can is ideal)

Round-nose pliers

Wire cutters

Rock tumbler and #60 silicon-carbide grit

Instructions

One
Tumble the glass pieces in a rock tumbler with coarse silicon carbide grit and water for 24 hours, or until the glass is frosted and the edges are smooth. (See page 36 for information on tumbling glass.)

Two
Make the horse-hair braid. Take an 18-inch-long (45.5-cm) hank of horse hair, approximately ¼ inch (.5 cm) in diameter. Divide the hank into three equal sections and braid it along the entire length. Tightly wrap the ends of the braid with the twine, knotting the twine to secure it. Saturate each end of the braid with craft glue to keep the strands of hair from pulling out. Set the braid aside and allow the glue to dry thoroughly. Then trim the hair flush with the end of the wrapped twine.

Three
Use the epoxy glue to glue the gold cylindrical end caps to each end of the braid, covering the wrapped twine.

Four
Cut two 3-inch (7.5-cm) lengths of black leather cord. To each of the four ends, attach a crimp end by wrapping the crimp ends around the cord and crushing each with the flat-nose pliers. Attach a jump ring to each of the four loops on the crimp ends. Attach one end of the one of the cords to the toggle, and one end of one of the cords to the bar clasp. Then attach the other ends of each cord to the loops on the cylindrical end caps.

Five
Using the craft drill and diamond-coated bit, drill a hole at the top of each of the 11 items which will hang from the horse-hair braid: seven pieces of glass; coconut shell; two pieces of bone; and the pebble. Using plastic putty, stick each item to the bottom of the shallow can before drilling. Make sure you use water to irrigate the drilling. (See the instructions for drilling hard materials on page 24.)

Six
Gather the components for the 11 sets of dangles. For each set, you will need: a piece of glass, coconut shell, bone, pebble; one bone bead; one hackberry seed; one gold bead; and 11 lengths of brass wire, each 5 inches (12.5 cm) long.

Seven
Before you assemble and attach these pieces to the braid, arrange them on a flat surface to determine their placement order around the braid. Then decide where you will attach these dangles to the horse-hair braid; the necklace shown has a dangle attached to every other bottom loop of braid.

Eight

To assemble and attach the dangles, begin by stringing a round bone bead on a piece of wire, positioning it at the center of the wire. Fold the wire in half; the bone bead will be at the bottom of the looped end and will act as a decorative stop bead for holding the glass, coconut shell, bone, or pebble. Insert the two free ends of wire through the hole in the piece of glass (or coconut shell, bone, or pebble). Next, holding the two wire ends together as one, string on a hackberry seed, then a gold bead. Using the round-nose pliers, make a single loop from the two ends of wire. Thread the ends together through a bottom loop on the braid. Using the serrated-jaw flat-nose pliers, wrap the two wires as one around the double-wire shaft three times. Trim the free ends of the wire using the wire cutters. Continue assembling and attaching until all 11 dangles are on the braid.

Stippled Sea Heart Pendant

The inlaid design on this sea heart pendant is made by drilling holes into which you insert head pins. By trimming and sanding the head pins, the design lies flush to the surface of the drift seed. With this technique you can create your own abstract design or a picture of your choice.

Materials

1 sea heart

Brass head pins, 1 inch (2.5 cm) in length

1 small screw eye

Tools

Sanding and polishing tools and equipment

Black felt-tip pen

Metallic gold pen

Craft drill with a set of small numbered drill bits

Epoxy glue

Wax paper

Toothpicks

Wire cutters

Aluminum oxide grinding wheel to fit the craft drill

Instructions

One

Following the specific instructions for sanding and polishing sea hearts on page 35, sand and polish the sea heart to a mirror finish.

Two

Choose the design you will use. You may want to make a few preliminary sketches first. Since the design is comprised of dots, it will help to draw your design by making a series of dots on paper with a black felt-tipped pen.

Three

Using the metallic gold pen pen, "dot" your design onto the sea heart, or draw your guidelines. You can also drill the holes freehand.

Four

Select a drill bit that corresponds to the diameter of the head pins you are using. (I use a #70 drill bit to accommodate most head pins.) With the craft drill and the selected bit, and following your design, drill the holes in the sea heart. Do not drill too deeply; drilling approximately 1/8 to 1/4 inch (.3-.5 cm) should be deep enough.

Five

Using a toothpick, mix the epoxy glue on the wax paper. Dip a head pin into the epoxy, then insert it into a hole in the sea heart. Continue inserting glue-dipped head pins into the sea heart until your design is complete. You may need to trim the head pins down to 1/8 inch (.3 cm) or so as you work to prevent getting tangled in them.

Six

When you have inserted all the head pins into the sea heart, set the sea heart aside for several hours to allow the epoxy to dry and harden. Then use the wire cutters to trim the head pins as close to their bases as you can.

Seven

With the aluminum oxide grinding wheel on the craft drill, grind down the protruding ends of the head pins until they are flush with the surface of the sea heart. Follow the safety precautions for grinding found on page 25. When the pins are flush, sand the surface of the sea heart with fine sandpaper (#600) until the surface is perfectly smooth. Then, if necessary, re-polish the surface by hand to a mirror finish using a jeweler's cloth or a cloth with jeweler's rouge on it. You can also use a craft drill with a buffing wheel that's been dipped in jeweler's rouge to polish the surface.

Eight

To finish, drill a small hole in the top of the sea heart. Use the craft drill and a drill bit that corresponds to the diameter of screw eye that you are using. Prepare a small amount of epoxy glue. Dip the screw eye into the epoxy, then insert the screw eye into the hole on the top of the sea heart. Allow the epoxy to dry thoroughly.

Sea Heart Locket

As a drift seed, the sea heart has a naturally hard, thick shell. When you remove the endosperm that's inside the seed, you're left with a hollow, protective case that's perfect for holding or carrying small items. This utilitarian property of drift seeds was once used to commercial advantage; the sea heart's cousin, the snuffbox bean, produces seeds that were made into snuffboxes before the advent of plastics.

Materials

1 sea heart

4 flat seeds approximately 3/16 inch (.4 cm) in diameter (shown here are Cana fistula seeds)

1 twig cross-section, approximately 3/8 inch (1 cm) in diameter and 3/16 inch (.4 cm) thick

1 royal poinciana seed, or other seed or bead approximately 1/4 inch (.5 cm) wide by 3/4 inch (2 cm) long

5 head pins, 1 inch (2.5 cm) in length (or longer)

1 piece of brown felt, approximately 1/2 x 1 1/2 inch (1.5 x 4 cm)

4 x 3 inch (10 x 7.5 cm) piece of felt

Craft glue

Strong thread, 10-inch (25.5 cm) length

Black elastic thread, 4-inch (10 cm) length

1 fold-over crimp end

Black sewing thread, 4-inch (10 cm) length

Hemp cord, 2 yards (1.8 m)

Tools

Craft drill with a set numbered drill bits

1/2 inch (1.5-cm) masking tape

Scissors

Vise

A 1/16-inch (.16-cm) drill bit for the craft drill

Metallic gold pen

Craft knife with a fine-tooth saw blade

Screwdriver

Wire cutters

Crimping pliers or flat-nose pliers

Instructions

One

From the numbered drill-bit set, select a drill bit that corresponds in size to the diameter of the head pins your are using (used here, #70). With that bit and the craft drill, drill holes through the flat sides of the four Cana fistula (or other) seeds. Using the same bit, drill a hole through the flat side of the twig cross-section. Again using the same bit, drill a hole in one end of the royal poinciana seed. Set the seeds aside.

Two

To prepare the sea heart for drilling and cutting, mark your cutting line with masking tape. First cut a 12-inch (30.5-cm) length of 1/2-inch (1.5-cm) masking tape in half to make two 1/4-inch-wide (.5 cm) strips. The top edge of the masking tape will by your guide for the cutting line, so make sure you have the tape positioned straight and exactly where you want the bean to open. Lay the piece of masking tape across the upper part of the sea heart at the cutting line, wrapping the tape around the back. To match the lid and bottom after the bean is cut, lay two strips of masking tape vertically across the horizontal masking tape and around the sea bean as guidelines.

Three

To protect the surface of the seed from being scratched by the jaws of the vise, wrap the seed in a small piece of felt before placing it in the vise. Tighten the jaws of the vise just enough to hold the seed securely; if you squeeze too tightly, the shell may crack. Just below the tape edge on both sides of the sea heart, use the craft drill with the 1/16-inch

(.16-cm) drill bit to drill a hole in each side where you will later attach the hemp cord.

FOUR

With the marker, mark where you will drill holes for attaching the seeds and twig cross-section. Since the twig will be in the center, mark that point first. Then mark two evenly spaced points on either side of the center point. With the small drill bit used in Step 1, drill holes at these points. Do not drill through the bean, only through the top side.

FIVE

To make the holes for stringing the elastic cord for the loop, use the $\frac{1}{16}$-inch (.16-cm) drill bit to drill two holes approximately $\frac{1}{4}$ inch (.5 cm) above the top edge of the masking tape. Center the hole above the hole for the twig cross-section.

SIX

Turn the seed over and drill four holes in the back of the seed for the felt-and-string hinge. To do this, first drill three holes in a row just below the bottom edge of the tape, centering the middle hole on the center point of the sea bean, and spacing the holes $\frac{3}{8}$ inch (1 cm) apart. Then drill one hole $\frac{1}{4}$ inch (.5 cm) above the edge of the masking tape, positioning it just above the middle hole in the row of three holes.

SEVEN

Using the craft knife with the fine-tooth saw blade, cut the bean slowly and carefully across the top edge of the strip of masking tape. To begin, angle the saw to cut the edges, then continue to cut at an angle at each end of the bean, until you have sawn clean through.

EIGHT

When the bean is cut, remove the endosperm by chipping it out using a small screwdriver. If the seed is fresh (and viable), the endosperm will be firmly attached to the sides and may take some time and patience.

NINE

Once the endosperm is removed, attach the four *Cana fistula* seeds and the twig to the sea heart with head pins. String each seed and the twig on a head pin, then thread the head pin through the holes you drilled in Step 4. Bend the free ends of the heads pins, which are now inside the sea heart, to secure them, trimming any excess wire with the wire cutters.

TEN

To make the felt-and-string hinge on the back, place the sea heart in the vise with the back side facing up. Use the vertical strips of tape to carefully line up the edges of each piece, top to bottom. Lay the $\frac{1}{2}$ x $1\frac{1}{2}$ inch (1.5 x 4 cm) felt rectangle on either side of the cut opening, covering the holes you drilled in Step 6. Using craft glue, glue the felt to the seed. Allow the glue to dry.

ELEVEN

When the glue is dry, take the locket out of the vise. Open the top to flex the felt a bit. To make the hinge stronger, use strong thread and a needle to lace the thread through the four holes and felt. Secure the ends of the thread with a strong knot inside the seed.

TWELVE

To make the elastic loop, thread one end of elastic cord through one hole in the top, then thread the other end into the other hole so both cord ends are inside the top of the locket. Determine the length of the elastic loop needed to go around the twig cross-section to hold the locket closed. To secure the ends of the elastic, attach a fold-over crimp end to both ends of the cord that are inside of the seed, crushing the crimp end with the flat-nose or crimping pliers. Trim the ends of the elastic.

THIRTEEN

With small needle and thread, attach the royal poinciana seed to the elastic loop, tying a small knot in the thread end.

FOURTEEN

Fold the hemp cord in half, then in half again. Place one end of the doubled cord through one of the side holes in the seed. Tie the ends in a knot inside the locket. Repeat for the other end of the hemp cord, adjusting the length of the cord as you desire before tying the knot inside the seed. Trim the cord ends.

WISTERIA EARRINGS

Stack a few chocolate-brown wisteria seeds with a few purchased beads for simple, but elegant, earrings.

MATERIALS

- *6 wisteria seeds*
- *2 silver head pins, 2 inches (5 cm) in length*
- *2 small silver beads*
- *2 melon-shaped silver beads*
- *2 disk-shaped silver beads*
- *2 small, round bone beads*
- *2 silver ear wires*
- *2 silver jump rings, 3mm in size*

Tools

- *Craft drill with a 1/16-inch (.16-cm) drill bit*
- *Round-nose pliers*
- *2 pairs of flat-nose pliers, one with smooht jaws, one with serrated jaws*
- *Wire cutters*

INSTRUCTIONS

ONE
Using the craft drill with the 1/16-inch (.16-cm) drill bit, drill holes through the flat faces of the six wisteria seeds.

TWO
On each 2-inch (5-cm) head pin, place the following in this order: a small silver bead; a melon-shaped silver bead; wisteria seeds; a disk-shaped silver bead; and a small bone bead.

THREE
With the round-nose pliers, make a loop at the top of each head pin, approximately 3/8 inch (1 cm) from the top of last bead. Hold the loop with the smooth-jaw flat-nose pliers while using the serrated-jaw flat-nose pliers to wrap the end of the wire that's below the loop around the pin's shaft. Trim any excess wire with the wire cutters.

FOUR
To finish, attach the ear wires to each earring loop with the 3mm jump rings.

SEASHELL STICK PIN

I found this iridescent seashell on a wonderful trip to the Pacific coast of Japan. I've also found similar shells on the California coast near La Jolla. Since the shells you find may not be exactly like this one, adapt this design for the shell you wish to feature. The bone beads came from a less exotic place, being the rescued scraps of a T-bone steak.

MATERIALS

2 bone beads, approximately ¼ inch (.5 cm) square

1 small clam shell

1 snail shell, or special shell to use as the central shell, approximately 1-1/4 inch (3 cm) in diameter

1 bamboo bead, approximately 1 inch (2.5 cm) long and ⅛ inch (.3 cm) in diameter

1 gold stick pin with a stop for the sharp end, 6 inches (15 cm) in length

2 flat, brass spacer beads, 4mm in diameter

1 piece of brown suede (optional), approximately ⅜ inch (1 cm) square

1 gold crimp bead

Tools

Craft drill with a diamond-coated drill bit

½ inch (1.5 cm) masking tape

Crimping pliers

Quick-drying glue

INSTRUCTIONS

ONE
Make the square bone beads by following the directions for working with bone found on pages 33-34.

TWO
Using the craft drill with the diamond-coated drill bit, drill holes through the bone beads, the clam shell, and your central shell, by following the instructions for drilling hard materials found on page 24. Determine the point for drilling your central shell before you drill by placing a strip of masking tape across the shell where you want the drill bit to enter and exit.

THREE
Make the bamboo bead by cutting a 1-inch (2.5-cm) length from a thin piece of bamboo that is approximately ⅛ inch (.3 cm) in diameter. Most of this bead will be inside the shell, and will help to hold the shell in place. If needed, make this bead longer to correspond to the length of your shell.

FOUR
Thread the beads and shell onto the stick pin in this order: a spacer bead; a bone bead; the piece of suede; the clam shell; your central shell; the bamboo bead, a bone bead, and two spacer beads.

FIVE
Move the beads and shells up, making the top bead fit snugly against the head of the stick pin. To hold the shells and beads in place, place a crimp bead on the stick pin beneath the last spacer bead. Then use the crimping pliers to crush it.

SIX
To keep the shell from rotating on the shaft of the stick pin, apply some quick-drying glue to the flat back of the shell at the point where it touches the bamboo bead.

Pebble and Coconut Pendant Necklace

Unusual pebbles or stones are bound to catch your eye when you are out looking for natural materials. Why not pick some of your favorites to incorporate into a jewelry design? Coconut makes a wonderful backing for displaying these treasures, and the brass wire, while serving to hold the pebbles in place, can add extra design interest by using different lacing patterns.

Materials

1 piece of coconut shell, approximately 1 x 2 inches (2.5 x 5 cm)

5 small, flat pebbles

1 flat piece of cow bone

Brass wire, 24-gauge

Black leather cord, 1mm in diameter, approximately 24 inches (61 cm)

2 flat brass beads

Black or brown felt, approximately the same size as the piece of coconut

Craft glue

1 round gold bead, 3mm in diameter

Tools

Sanding and polishing equipment

Craft drill with a ¹⁄₁₆-inch (.16-cm) drill bit

Black felt-tipped marker (optional)

Diamond-coated drill bit for a craft drill

Plastic putty

Shallow can (a cat food can works well)

Wire cutters

Flat-nose pliers

Scissors

INSTRUCTIONS

ONE

Sand, polish, and buff the coconut piece. I polish many coconut pieces at one time in a rock tumbler with water and #100 silicon-carbide grit. If sanding by hand, begin by using a coarse-grit sand-paper, then use progressively finer grits until reaching the desired smoothness. Buff the piece by hand using a jeweler's cloth, or with a buffing wheel dipped in jeweler's rouge on a craft drill.

TWO

Using the craft drill with the ¹⁄₁₆-inch (.16-cm) drill bit, drill a hole in the top of the coconut piece to accommodate the leather cord.

THREE

Decide where you will place the pebbles and bone on the piece of coconut. For accurate place-ment later on, it's helpful to out-line them on the coconut using a black felt-tipped marker.

FOUR

Before you drill the holes in the pebbles and bone, decide how you will lash the pebbles to the coconut with wire. For instance,

each of the pebbles and the cow bone shown on the pendant has drill holes that are placed differ-ently: the black pebble has a hole at each end; the other peb-ble has four holes for crisscross-ing the wire; and the bone bead has four holes for parallel lacing. You'll drill the other three peb-bles through the middle of their flat sides for stringing.

FIVE

Using the diamond-coated drill bit, and following your lacing patterns, drill through the peb-bles and bone. Follow the direc-tions for drilling hard materials found on page 24. Begin by placing the plastic putty in the shallow can, then pressing a pebble or piece of bone into the putty. Pour water into the can to just cover the putty and the material to be drilled.

SIX

Place one of the drilled pebbles on top of the coconut piece; this is where outlining as described in Step 3 comes in handy. While holding the pebble in place with one hand, ldrill through the already-drilled pebble or bone holes and through the coconut piece. If you cannot keep the pebble from slipping around, secure it temporarily to the coconut with a piece of plastic putty. Repeat for the other peb-ble and the piece of bone.

SEVEN

Using the brass wire, lash the pebbles and bone to the coconut by lacing the wire through the holes. You can use one continu-ous piece of wire, or you can use shorter pieces of wire for each pebble. Using the flat-nose pli-ers, tightly twist the wire ends together at the back of the piece

of coconut. Flatten the twisted ends flush to the coconut, so they won't stick out.

EIGHT

Cut a piece of felt large enough to cover the back of the piece of coconut. Using craft glue, glue the felt onto the back of the piece of coconut and allow to dry thoroughly.

NINE

To attach the cord to the coconut pendant, use a lark's head hitch knot. To do this, begin by folding the cord in half. Thread the fold, front to back, through the hole at the top of the coconut piece. Pass the two free ends of the cord through the loop made by the fold, pulling the two ends to tighten the loop. Measure approximately 2 inches (5 cm) up from pendant on both sides of the cord, and tie an overhand knot in each side. On each side, string a pebble and a flat bead. Make a second overhand knot just above the flat beads to keep the bead and pebble from mov-ing on the cord.

TEN

To close the necklace, make a toggle and loop in the leather ends. Decide on the desired length for the necklace, then add 2 inches (5 cm) for the loop. Cut away any excess cord. Tie an overhand knot at one end of the cord, approximately 1 inch (2.5 cm) from the end. String the last pebble and the gold bead on the cord, tying another overhand knot just above the gold bead to secure. On the other end of the cord make a loop that will be large enough to fit around the pebble and gold bead. Knot the leather cord securely and trim.

LONG NECKLACE WITH A PRICKLY PALM SEED

This is one of the first necklaces I made using seeds mixed with a miscellany of materials, including some simple beads that I fashioned from polymer clay. This man-made material is easy to use and can enhance your design options when looking for complementary components for your natural jewelry. I made this necklace long enough to double over, or it can be worn at its full length. You can substitute any intersting seed for the central bead.

MATERIALS

Polymer clay in white, beige, dark red, and navy blue to make 20 flat polymer clay beads, approximately ¼ x ½ inch (.5 x 1.5 cm) and 10 round polymer clay beads, approximately ½ inch (1.5 cm) in diameter

1 Prickly Palm seed

2 Pindo Palm seeds

60 Mescal beans

1 driftwood stick, approximately ⅜ inch (1 cm) in diameter

2 small pieces of coconut shell with fiber removed, each approximately ⅜ x ½ inch (1 x 1.5 cm)

11 bamboo sections, each approximately ³⁄₁₆ inch (.4 cm) in diameter (or smaller) and approximately ½ inch (1.5 cm) long

60 round gold beads, 3mm in diameter

38 rice-shaped gold beads

16 wooden beads, 8mm in diameter

4 yards (3.6 m) of beading string

Craft glue

Tools

Craft knife

Craft drill with a ¹⁄₁₆-inch (.16-cm) drill bit

Fine-tooth saw or cut-off wheels to fit craft drill

Woodburning tool (optional)

Scissors

Needle to fit beading string

INSTRUCTIONS

ONE
Make the polymer clay beads. For the flat beads, begin by making a "jelly roll" by layering sheets of beige, dark red, and navy blue clay. Then roll them up together to make a ½-inch-diameter (1.5 cm) roll. Using a sharp craft knife, slice the roll into ¼-inch-wide (.5 cm) slices. To make the round polymer clay beads, roll pieces of the remaining jelly roll with pieces of white polymer clay. Following the clay manufacturer's instructions, bake the beads and allow to cool.

TWO
Drill all the seeds and polymer clay beads using the craft drill and the ¹⁄₁₆-inch (.16 cm) drill bit. Drill through the middle of the flat side of each of the coconut shell pieces. Drill through the narrow edge of the polymer clay beads.

THREE
With the fine-tooth saw, cut the driftwood twig into eight cross sections, each about ¼ inch (.5 cm) thick. Drill holes through the "face" of each section. If desired, use a woodburnig tool to decorate these sections with dots, dashes, and stripes.

FOUR
Following the photograph as a guide for the stringing pattern, use the beading thread and needle to string the seeds, beads, twigs, and bamboo sections as shown. Begin by stringing one small piece of coconut, one bamboo section, and one piece of coconut. Tie the ends with several strong knots. Trim any excess thread. You may want to dot the knots with craft glue for extra security.

Spiral Seashell Necklace

Wrapping a spiral shell with wire embellishes one of nature's most perfect designs. If you prefer, you can also hang this simple pendant from a chain.

Materials

Spiral seashell with deep grooves (this one was purchased)

Brass, copper, or silver wire, in either 18-, 20-, or 24-gauge

Quick-drying or epoxy glue (optional)

Tools

Flat-nose pliers

Round-nose pliers

Wire cutters

Instructions

One
Leaving approximately a 1-inch (2.5-cm) end of wire free, start at the bottom (large end) of the shell and wrap the wire around it. Wrap the wire as tightly as you can, placing it in the shell's grooves (the sutures), until you get to the top. Wind the wire tightly around the top two or three times.

Two
Use the round-nose pliers to make a loop in the wire at the top of the shell. Wrap the ends of the wire around the wire shaft a few times and trim with wire cutters.

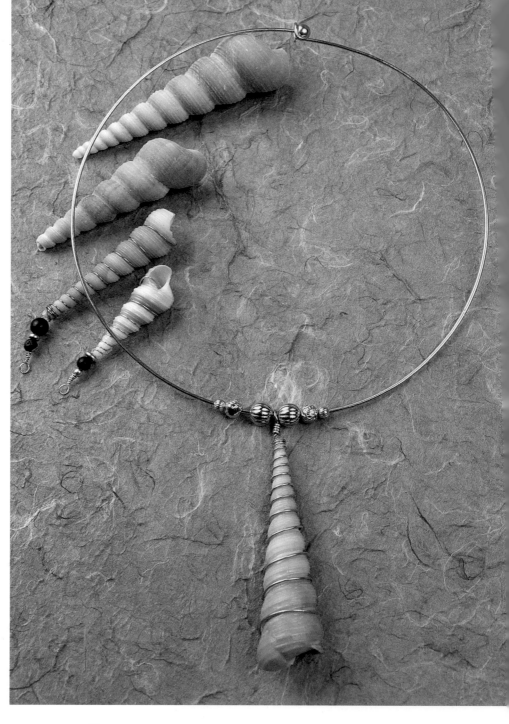

Three
To finish, tuck the wire end that's at the bottom of the shell into the inside lip of shell. To prevent the wire from loosening, pull the wire as tight as the shell will bear. If necessary, secure the wire to the shell at the top with a drop or two of strong, quick-drying glue or epoxy, and allow to dry thoroughly.

Four
You may want to embellish this pendant with additional beads or seeds. To do so, string beads or seeds onto the wire at the top of the shell before you make the loop in the wire.

ACORN EARRINGS

Acorns make versatile beads. Their woody shells can be polished or stained with leather dye to create different looks for your jewelry. The acorns used for these earrings do not have any added surface treatment, leaving their natural, rich brown color to offset the gold findings.

MATERIALS

SIMPLE DANGLE

2 acorns, without caps

2 dangle pins, 2 inches (5 cm) in length

4 round gold beads, 4mm in diameter

2 ear wires

2 jump rings, 4mm in size

FANCY DANGLE

2 acorns, without caps

2 head pins, 2 inches (5 cm) in length

6 small, flat brass spacer beads

4 fancy gold bead caps

2 barrel-shaped gold beads

2 ear wires

2 jump rings, 3mm in size

Tools

Craft drill with a 1/16-inch (.16-cm) drill bit

Round-nose pliers

2 pairs of flat-nose pliers, one with smooth jaws, one with serrated jaws

Wire cutters

INSTRUCTIONS

SIMPLE DANGLE

ONE
Using the craft drill with the 1/16-inch (.16-cm) drill bit, drill holes lengthwise through the two acorns.

TWO
On each dangle pin, place a round gold bead, an acorn, and another round bead.

THREE
With the round-nose pliers, make a loop at the top of each head pin, approximately ¼ inch (.5 cm) from the top of last bead. Hold the loop with the smooth-jaw flat-nose pliers while using the serrated-jaw flat-nose pliers to wrap the end of the wire that's below the loop around the pin's shaft. Trim any excess wire with the wire cutters.

FOUR
To finish, attach the ear wires to the dangle pins with jump rings.

FANCY DANGLE

ONE
Using the craft drill with the 1/16-inch (.16-cm) drill bit, drill holes lengthwise through the two acorns.

TWO
On each head pin place the following in this order: flat spacer bead; bead cap; acorn; flat spacer bead; barrel-shaped bead; flat spacer bead.

THREE
With the round-nose pliers, make a loop at the top of each head pin, approximately ¼ inch (.5 cm) from the top of last bead. Hold the loop with the smooth-jaw flat-nose pliers while using the serrated-jaw flat-nose pliers to wrap the end of the wire that's below the loop around the pin's shaft. Trim any excess wire with the wire cutters.

FOUR
To finish, attach the head pins to the ear wires with the jump rings.

Bottle Glass and Chicken Bone Necklace

Use glass that you find on the beach, or recycle pieces of broken bottles that would otherwise litter your environment. You'll find that hollow chicken bones make interesting and easy-to-string beads.

Materials

1 piece of blue bottle glass

2 chicken leg bones (from drumsticks)

1 round bone bead, 3mm in diameter (purchased)

2 flat metal spacer beads

3 oblong silver beads

1 smaller piece of bottle glass (to make the clasp)

1 yard (.9 m) of black leather cord, 1mm in diameter

Silver wire, 28-gauge

Tools

Fine-tooth saw, or round saw blade to fit the craft drill

Craft drill and 1/16-inch (.16-cm) drill bit

Sandpaper, or sanding drum to fit the craft drill

Diamond-coated drill bit

Scissors

Wire cutters

Round-nose pliers

Instructions

One
If necessary, use a rock tumbler to smooth and frost the glass (see page 36).

Two
Clean and disinfect the chicken bones (see pages 33-34). Using the fine-tooth saw or round saw blade for the craft drill, saw the chicken bones into six beads, each approximately 1/4 inch (.5 cm) wide. Choose one of these as the center bead, and drill a hole through the flat face of the bead using the 1/16-inch (.16-cm) drill bit on the craft drill. Use the sandpaper or sanding drum for the craft drill to smooth any rough edges from the bone beads.

Three
Following the instructions for drilling hard materials on page 24, use the diamond-coated drill bit in the craft drill to drill a hole in the top of the blue bottle glass. Then drill a hole through the center of the smaller piece of glass.

Four
Cut a 30-inch (76-cm) piece of the 1mm leather cord.

Five
Using the photo as a guide, string the beads and bone onto the leather cord as follows: one oblong silver bead; two bone beads; center bone bead with drilled hole; two bone beads; one oblong silver bead. Tie a knot above each of the two oblong silver beads to keep them from slipping on the leather cord.

Six
To make the pendant, begin by cutting a 10-inch (25.5-cm) length of silver wire. Bend the wire in half. Insert the bent end through both drilled holes in the center bone bead. Then string these beads as follows onto the silver wire: one round bone bead; one flat metal bead; one oblong silver bead; one chicken bone bead; one flat spacer bead.

Seven
Insert the two strands of wire through the hole in the blue glass, then loop them over the top of the glass. Use the pliers to wrap the wire ends around the shaft a few times, trimming any excess wire with the wire cutters.

Eight
To make the toggle clasp, first decide on the desired necklace length, adding 2 inches (5 cm) to accommodate the toggle loop. Thread the smaller piece of glass onto one end of the leather cord. Tie an overhand knot above the glass to secure it. Trim the leather cord approximately 1/8 inch (.3 cm) from the knot. On the other end of the leather cord, make a loop large enough for the glass toggle to fit through. Knot the ends securely and trim.

Blue Chinaberry Necklace with Two Pairs of Earrings

Chinaberries are easy to dye, making them a versatile member of the jewelry-plant family. By using liquid or powdered fabric dye, which you can purchase in a grocery store, you can quickly change these naturally soft-beige beads into any color that suits your mood.

Materials

Necklace

104 chinaberries dyed blue

1 chinaberry dyed purple (optional)

52 flat, bleached-wood beads, 8mm in diameter (purchased)

52 round, bleached-wood beads, 6mm in diameter (purchased)

1 round gold bead, 3mm in diameter

Beading thread

Craft glue

Dangle Earrings

2 chinaberries, dyed blue

2 flat, bleached-wood beads, 8mm in diameter (purchased)

2 round, bleached-wood beads, 6mm in diameter (purchased)

2 head pins, 2 inches (5 cm) long

2 ear wires

2 jump rings, 3mm in size

Hoop earrings

6 chinaberries, dyed blue

8 round, bleached-wood beads, 8 mm in diameter (purchased)

2 earring hoops

2 ear wires

2 jump rings, 3 mm in size

Tools

Craft drill with a $\frac{1}{16}$-inch (.16-cm) drill bit

Scissors

Needle to fit beading thread

Flat-nose pliers

Crimping pliers

Round-nose pliers

Instructions

Necklace

ONE
Dye the chinaberries following the instructions on page 44 for dyeing melon and squash seeds. When the chinaberries are in the dye bath, check them periodically for color; remember that wet chinaberries will look darker than they will once dried. Allow the chinaberries to dry thoroughly before drilling.

TWO
Starting at the flat end of each seed, use the craft drill with the $\frac{1}{16}$-inch (.16-cm) drill bit to drill lengthwise holes in the chinaberries.

THREE
Using the beading thread and needle, alternate stringing chinaberries and wooden beads following the pattern shown in the photograph. To finish, use a square knot to tie the two ends of beading thread together. Do not trim the ends.

FOUR
Thread both ends of thread together on the needle. Using the needle and both ends of thread as one, string a flat wooden bead, the purple chinaberry, another flat wooden bead, and the 3mm gold bead. Tie the thread off with a knot, then dot the knot with craft glue.

Hoop Earrings

ONE
Using the photograph as your guide, string the round beads and blue chinaberries as shown.

TWO
Close the hoop, use crimping pliers to crush the metal around the wire end of the hoop to secure it.

THREE
Connect an ear wire to each hoop with a jump ring.

Dangle Earrings

ONE
On each of the 2-inch (5-cm) head pins, place a 2mm gold bead, a flat wooden bead, a blue chinaberry, a round wooden bead, and another 2mm gold bead. Use round-nose pliers to make a loop at the top of the head pin, then wrap the end of the head pin around the head pin's shaft.

TWO
Connect an ear wire to each head pin loop with a jump ring.

ElEPHANT EAR AND BETEl NUT NECklACE

Elephant ear seeds, with their dark brown centers surrounded by a light brown ring, present their own unique design element to this necklace. The betel-nut dangles are easily attached to the necklace by gold bails, which are strung, along with the seeds, onto the beading thread.

MATERIAls

26 elephant ear seeds

Beading thread

2 bead end caps with loops

5 gold bails

5 dangle pins, 2 inches (5 cm) in length

10 round gold beads, 4mm in diameter

5 betel nut beads (purchased)

5 jump rings, 4mm in size

1 toggle-and-bar clasp

2 jump rings, 3mm in size

Craft glue

Tools

Craft drill with a ¹⁄₁₆-inch (.16-cm) drill bit

Scissors

Needle to fit beading thread

Round-nose pliers

2 pairs of flat-nose pliers, one with smooth jaws, one with serrated jaws

Wire cutters

INSTRUCTIONS

ONE
Using the craft drill and the ¹⁄₁₆-inch (.16-cm) drill bit, drill holes lengthwise in the elephant ear seeds.

TWO
Cut a 30-inch (76-cm) length of beading thread. Tie a knot on one end, then string on a bead end cap to hide the knot. Thread the needle on the other end of the thread. Following the photograph as your guide, string the elephant ear seeds and bails onto the thread, placing a bail after every three seeds. When you're finished stringing, thread on the second bead end cap, take up slack in the thread, and tie several knots. Place a dot of craft glue on the knot to secure.

THREE
Make the five dangle sets to hang from the five bails. On a 2-inch (5-cm) dangle pin, place a gold bead, a betel nut, and another gold bead. With the round-nose pliers, make a loop in the end of the dangle pin, approximately ¼ inch (.5 cm) from the top of the last bead. Holding the wire loop with the smooth-jaw flat-nose pliers, use the serrated-jaw flat-nose pliers to wrap the end of the dangle pin that's beneath the loop around the pin's shaft. Trim any excess wire with the wire cutters. Repeat for the remaining four dangles. Attach each dangle to each bail with a 4mm jump ring.

FOUR
With the 3mm jump rings, attach the toggle-and-bar clasp to the loops on the bead end caps.

Coconut and Bamboo Barrette

Utilize the natural curve of the coconut shell to make these simple hair barrettes. The coconut shell not only provides a strong material, it also offers some interesting surface markings that will appear as you polish.

Materials

Curved piece of coconut shell, approximately 5 inches (12.5 cm) long measured on the curve

Bamboo, a length approximately 5½ inches (14 cm) long by 1/16 inch (.16 cm) wide

Craft glue

Raffia

Tools

Craft drill with sanding barrel

Sandpaper, in coarse (#150), medium (#200), and fine (#400) grits

Buffing wheel for a craft drill, or a jeweler's cloth

Jeweler's rouge

Vise

Power drill with a 5/16-inch (.75-cm) drill bit

Instructions

One

Using coarse sandpaper, sand off the coconut fiber and smooth the edges of the piece of coconut. Sand the outer surface of the coconut with coarse sandpaper until smooth. Finish sanding and smoothing the coconut with medium- and then fine-grit sandpaper.

Two

If you have a buffing wheel for your craft drill, dip the buffing wheel in jeweler's rouge, then apply it to the surface of the coconut piece, buffing and polishing until the surface is shiny. Or buff and polish by hand, using a jeweler's cloth.

Three

Place the coconut piece securely in a vise. Use the power drill with the 5/16-inch (.75-cm) drill bit to drill a hole in each end of the coconut. Finish each hole by sanding the sharp edges with the craft drill and the sanding barrel. For decorative purposes, you may want to use the sanding barrel to make a depression on the edges of the holes that are toward the barrette's edge. Re-polish any areas that may need it.

Four

Using the craft drill and sanding barrel, smooth and curve the ends of the bamboo stick. Then clean, buff, and polish the stick.

Five

To keep the ends of the bamboo stick from fraying, lay a thin coat of craft glue on the insides of each end (on the softer, pale side of the stick).

Six

If desired for added decoration, wrap and tie some raffia around the barrette.

Seven

As a variation, use the craft drill with a saw attachment to carve out sections of the coconut piece before you begin sanding its outer surface. Be sure to leave a central bar of the coconut shell, approximately ¼ inch (.5 cm) wide, for securing the stick as it passes under the hair. You can also drill small holes for lacing wire to embellish the design. Use an African porcupine quill as the stick, cutting it to size and sanding the ends smooth as you did in Step 4 for the bamboo stick. Tie raffia to the central bar for added decoration.

Green Glass Earrings

You may be lucky enough to find two pieces of similar beach glass to make this pair of earrings. If not, use a rock tumbler to frost and smooth glass pieces for this project. For a unique pair of earrings, use two pieces of glass that are dissimilar.

Materials

2 pieces of green glass

2 bagpod seeds

2 small, flat brass beads

8 jump rings, 3mm in size

6 dangle pins, each 2 inches (5 cm) long

2 ear wires

Tools

Craft drill with a diamond-coated drill bit

#61 drill bit for the craft drill

Round-nose pliers

Flat-nose pliers

Wire cutters

Instructions

One

If needed, use a rock tumbler to smooth and frost the pieces of glass (see page 36).

Two

Drill a hole at the top of each glass piece, using the diamond-coated bit. Make sure you irrigate the drill bit with water as you work. (See page 24 for the instructions for drilling hard materials.)

Three

At the bottom of each piece of glass, drill three holes in a straight row and spaced evenly. Attach a jump ring to each hole.

Four

Using the #61 drill bit on the craft drill, drill the two bagpod seeds lengthwise.

Five

On each of two dangle pins, place a bagpod seed and a small, flat brass bead. Using the round-nose pliers, make a loop at the top of each of the dangle pins, beginning approximately ½ inch (1.5 cm) from the top of the brass bead. Using the flat-nose pliers, wrap the wire ends around each pin shaft several times, then trim any excess with the wire cutters.

Six

Make loops at the top of each of the remaining four dangle pins, beginning the loop approximately 1 inch (2.5 cm) below the top of the dangle pin. Wrap the wire end around the pin's shaft. Trim any excess wire ends with the wire cutters.

Seven

To finish, assemble the earrings. Attach an ear wire to the top of each glass piece with a jump ring. Then attach the three dangle pins to the jump rings at the bottom of each piece of glass, making the pin with the bagpod seed the middle dangle.

COCONUT BARRETTE WITH SILVER WIRE AND BEADS

Silver wire and black leather cord finish the edge of this piece of coconut shell. By drilling holes, you can easily attach the silver beads and palm seeds that embellish this handsome barrette.

Materials

1 piece of coconut shell, approximately 3 x 2½ inches (5 x 6.5 cm)

Sterling silver wire, 2 feet (61 cm) of 22-gauge (I used square wire for this project)

Black leather cord, 1 foot (30.5 cm)

3 head pins, 2 inches (5 cm) long

6 silver beads of various sizes and shapes

2 small brown seeds (shown here are Mexican Fan Palm seeds)

Epoxy glue

Craft glue

Metal barrette clasp

Tools

Polishing and sanding equipment

Craft drill with a #61 or a ¹⁄₁₆-inch (.16-cm) drill bit (or smaller to fit the wire)

Needle-nose pliers

Wire cutters

Wax paper

Toothpicks

Clamp

Instructions

One

Sand and polish the piece of coconut shell. You can tumble the coconut piece in a rock tumbler until smooth (see page 65). Or, sand by hand starting with coarse sandpaper (#60-100), then using progressively finer grits of sandpaper until smooth. If you have a buffing wheel for your craft dill, dip the buffing wheel in jeweler's rouge, then apply it to the surface of the coconut piece, buffing and polishing until the surface is shiny. Or, buff and polish by hand, using a jeweler's cloth.

Two

Using the craft drill and the #61 or ¹⁄₁₆-inch (.16-cm) drill bit, drill holes in the perimeter of the coconut shell, spacing each hole approximately ⅛ inch (.3 cm) apart.

Three

Hold a section of the black leather cord against the edge of the coconut piece. With your other hand, and using an overhand whip stitch, thread the silver wire through the holes, catching the cord in the loops of wire as you work around the edge of the piece. Make sure you pull the wire snug to the cord after each stitch. Do not pull too tightly or the wire will deform the cord.

Four

To finish the lacing, cut the leather cord with the wire cutters so that the ends are flush. Make sure the cord ends are secure under a wire stitch. You may need to put a drop of craft glue on the joint made by the cord ends to help hold them together. Twist the ends of the wire together on the back of the coconut shell, pressing the twisted wire flat against the back with the needle-nose pliers.

Five

Drill seven holes in a row across the top edge of the coconut shell, approximately ⅜ inch (1 cm) away from the leather cord and wire.

Six

Make three sets of beads, each consisting of two silver beads strung on a head pin. Thread one of each of the three head pins through the first, fourth, and seventh holes. To secure the bead sets, use the needle-nose pliers to bend and twist the ends of the head pins together on the back of the coconut shell.

Seven

Drill holes in palm seeds, widthwise, with the #61 drill bit. To string the palm seeds, thread the wire through the second hole, place a palm seed on the wire, and take the wire back through the third hole to the back of the coconut. Twist the ends of the wire together. Do the same with another piece of wire and a palm seed, stringing the wire through the fifth and sixth holes. You can also attach both palm seeds using one continuous piece of wire, twisting the two ends of the wire together at the back of the coconut piece. Flatten all wire ends to the back of the coconut shell.

Eight

Using a toothpick, mix a small amount of epoxy glue on a piece of wax paper, then use another toothpick to apply it to the back of the coconut shell. Attach the metal barrette clasp, holding it in place with a clamp until the glue is thoroughly dry.

Pindo Palm Amulet Bracelet

Amulets are good-luck charms. Some cultures and religions have archetypal amulets or talismans that represent certain deities or concepts. But an amulet need not be assigned qualities or powers by others; you can choose your own objects that have meaning for you, as I've done here. By using memory wire, which retains its shape, you will create a bracelet that you can enjoy for many years.

Materials

40 pindo palm seeds

9 items for amulets (shown here are: twig section, lotus seed, blue gum eucalyptus pod, jojoba bean, jujube, giant Atlantic cockle, large gold bead, sea snail shell, and bamboo)

9 cylindrical end caps (in sizes to fit your amulets)

Epoxy glue

9 jump rings, 8mm in size

Bracelet memory wire, 22 inches (56 cm)

Tools

Craft drill with a 1/16-inch (.16-cm) drill bit

Wax paper

Toothpicks

Flat-nose pliers

Round-nose pliers

Wire cutters

Instructions

ONE

The pindo palm seeds used in this bracelet were smoothed by tumbling them in a rock tumbler for a few days with #60 silicon carbide grit and water. Although these seeds are left with a matte finish for this project, you can polish them by hand or in a rock tumbler to make them as glossy as you desire.

TWO

Using the craft drill with the 1/16-inch (.16-cm) drill bit, drill holes in pindo palm seeds lengthwise.

THREE

To attach the amulets to the end caps, use a toothpick to mix a small amount of epoxy glue on a piece of wax paper. Use another toothpick to apply the epoxy to the amulets, then attach the end caps to them. Allow the epoxy to dry and harden thoroughly before using the flat-nose pliers to attach the jump rings to the end-cap loops.

FOUR

With the round-nose pliers, make a small loop at one end of the memory wire to keep the seeds and amulets from sliding off. String the pindo palm seeds and amulets onto the memory wire. This bracelet has an amulet after every four palm seeds.

FIVE

Once you've strung the amulets and seeds, trim the memory wire with the wire cutters, leaving a 1/2-inch (1.5-cm) end. To finish, use the round-nose pliers to make a small loop on this end to secure the beads and amulets.

Twig Earrings

Look for interesting twigs for making earrings. Shown here are the stems of flower stalks from the palmetto tree. You can adapt this idea to whatever you find, since end caps come in a range of sizes. You can also carve and whittle twigs into simple shapes.

Materials

> 6 thin twigs
>
> 6 small gold end caps
>
> 6 silver jump rings, 3mm in size
>
> 2 silver jump rings, 6mm in size
>
> 2 ear wires
>
> Epoxy glue

Tools

> Scissors or pruning shears
>
> Wax paper
>
> Toothpicks
>
> Flat-nose pliers

Instructions

One

Cut six lengths of twig, each the same length. Don't trim them to size yet; wait until the earrings are assembled.

Two

Mix a small amount of epoxy glue on the wax paper. Using a toothpick, apply the glue to one end of each twig and attach an end cap. Allow the glue to dry and harden.

Three

Using the flat-nose pliers, attach a 3mm jump ring to each end cap. Then use these jump rings to slip three twigs onto each 6mm jump ring. Attach an ear wire to each 6mm jump ring to complete your earrings.

Four

Depending on the length of earring you desire, trim the ends of the twigs accordingly. For the earrings shown here, I cut the three twigs in different lengths for added interest.

Five

If needed for strength, you can coat the twigs with epoxy, but they will look unnaturally shiny if you do so.

Lightning Whelk and Coconut Earrings

Several years ago, I kept saltwater aquariums with animals that I collected from the surf of Texas coastal waters. One of the treasures I found was a group of eggs laid by a female Lightning Whelk (Busycon contrarium), a large American marine snail. The eggs consist of a string of soft, leathery capsules, each of which contains up to 100 baby snails—each with its own tiny shell. (These eggs, by the way, would not have survived being washed up on shore due to desiccation or attack by predators.)

I eventually had a hundred or so hatchlings in my aquarium, but many of the offspring were eaten by their cannibalistic siblings. These two shells belonged to the surviving brood of whelks and thrived for a month or two. Another "baby" from this group lived for four years in my tank and grew to a size of 2 inches (5 cm).

Materials

2 pieces of coconut shell, each approximately ¾ x 1 inch (2 x 2.5 cm)

2 tiny lightning whelk shells, or 2 similar small shells

2 earring backs and clutches

Epoxy glue

Spray enamel or varnish (optional)

Tools

Sandpaper or rock trumbler

#100 silicon-carbide grit

Jeweler's cloth or buffing wheel for a craft drill

Jeweler's rouge

Wax paper

Toothpicks

Left- and Right-Handed Seashells

Snail shells coil to the right (dextral) or to the left (sinistral). One of the rare left-handed shells of the world is a native American gastropod called a lightning whelk, or left-handed whelk. Its scientific name is Busycon contrarium pulleyi. No one knows why a gastropod is left- or right-handed.

To tell if a snail shell is right- or left-handed, hold the shell with the opening facing you and the top of the shell upright. The top is where the shell begins to coil and often has a point. If the opening is on the left as you look at the shell, it's a left-handed shell; if the opening is on the right, it's a right-handed shell.

Instructions

One

Sand, polish, and buff the coconut pieces. I polish many coconut pieces at one time in a rock tumbler with water and #100 silicon-carbide grit. If sanding by hand, begin by using a coarse-grit sandpaper, then use progressively finer grits until reaching the desired smoothness. You can either leave the coconut pieces with a flat finish, or buff them to achieve a polished look. If buffing by hand, use a jeweler's cloth. If you have a craft drill, use the buffing wheel dipped in jeweler's rouge to buff and polish.

Two

Using a toothpick, mix a small amount of epoxy glue on wax paper. Using another toothpick, apply the glue to attach a whelk to each piece of coconut. Then glue an earring back to each piece of coconut. Allow the glue to dry and harden.

Three

If desired, spray the earrings with clear enamel or varnish.

SHARK
TOOTH
EARRINGS

These two teeth were among many others I found on the upper beach at Amelia Island, Florida. Because they are often hard to spot when beachcombing, it may take you a while to collect enough sharks' teeth for making jewelry. But don't wait until you get a matched pair; two slightly different teeth make a handsome and unique pair of earrings.

Materials

- *2 shark teeth*
- *1 piece of 18-gauge silver-plated wire, 12 inches (30.5 cm) long*
- *2 silver-plated jump rings, 4mm in size*
- *2 silver-plated connectors (optional)*
- *2 silver ear wires*

Tools

- *Flat-nose pliers*
- *Round-nose pliers*
- *Wire cutters*

Instructions

ONE

Cut two pieces of silver-plated wire, each about 6 inches (15 cm) long.

TWO

To wrap each tooth, first hold a tooth in the center of one of the pieces of wire with the wire on the front side of the tooth. When you have a good grip with one hand, use the other hand to twist the wire as follows: take one free end of the wire and bend it toward the back of the tooth; bring this same wire end to the center of the back of the tooth; then bring this wire end forward and make a loop around the "horn" of one side of the tooth; bring the wire back to the center of the back of the tooth. Repeat with the other end of the wire on the other side of the tooth. The earring on the left in the photo below shows how the completed wrapping looks on the front, and the earring on the right shows the wrapping on the back.

THREE

When you have looped the wire over both "horns" of the tooth and each wire end is in the back of the tooth, then twist the two ends tightly together one time.

FOUR

Straighten the two ends of the wire, so that they point upwards from the top of the tooth. Using the wire cutters, trim both ends of the wire flush, approximately ½ inch (2 cm) away from the top of the tooth.

FIVE

With the round-nose pliers, bend both of the wire ends toward the front of the earring, forming a loop. Shape the loop with the round-nose and flat-nose pliers, so that the loops are even and pressed close together.

SIX

Repeat this process with the other tooth and piece of wire. Using the jump rings, attach an ear wire to each loop at the top of the earrings (or, if using decorative connectors, attach them to the tooth wires and ear wires).

Front   Back

TWIG BARRETTE

I used woody twigs from a rose bush—with the thorns cut off— to make this barrette. Together, the twigs make a tidy bundle, and their warm, red-brown color provides a nice complement to the brass wire.

MATERIALS

Several thin twigs, each approximately 5 inches (12.5 cm) long

Freshly stripped elder bark

Brass wire, 22- or 24-gauge

Barrette clip, 2¾ inches (7 cm) long

Clear nylon thread or fishing line

Tools

Scissors

Pocket or whittling knife

2 heavyweight rubber bands

Wire cutters

Embroidery needle with an eye that fits the thread

Needle-nose or flat-nose pliers

Clear spray enamel or varnish

INSTRUCTIONS

ONE
Use wire cutters or a sharp knife to trim the ends of the twigs diagonally. When finished, you want each twig to be approximately 4 inches (10 cm) long.

TWO
Bundle the twigs together, securing the bundle on each end with a heavyweight rubber band.

THREE
To make a rope from elder bark, strip a piece of fresh, wet bark approximately ½ inch (1.5 cm) wide by 12 inches (30.5 cm) long off of an elderberry stem. (You can substitute the bark from any sapling whose bark strips off easily.) Divide the piece of bark into at least three long strips. Tie the strips together at one end, then roll them together on your thigh until they are tightly twisted together.

FOUR
Working while the bark is still damp, wrap the rope diagonally around the twig bundle, tucking the ends of the bark under the rubber bands at either end.

FIVE
Cut two pieces of brass wire, each approximately 7 inches (18 cm) long. Wrap the wire around the two ends of the bundle, making sure you catch the ends of the bark rope to secure. Using the pliers, twist the two ends of each piece of wire securely together, tucking them into the bundle to hide the ends. Remove the rubber bands.

SIX
To attach the barrette back, thread a sturdy embroidery needle with clear nylon thread or fishing line. Sew the barrette back to the bundle, poking the needle through the bundle of twigs several times until secure. Trim the thread ends, and any loose ends of wire or bark.

SEVEN
To finish, allow the bark rope to dry completely, then apply a coat of clear spray enamel or varnish.

Kentucky Coffee Tree and Gingko Seed Earrings

The large size and light weight of the gingko and coffee tree seeds make them ideal earring material. With them, you can create earrings that are both comfortable and dramatic. Look for earring findings that provide more hanging capabilities, and you can add as many dangles as you dare!

Materials

(will make one pair of earrings)

2 gingko seeds

2 Kentucky coffee tree seeds, polished & buffed

4 round gold beads, 6mm in diameter (for the pair below)

4 round gold beads, 3mm in diameter (for the pair below)

8 round gold beads, 3mm in diameter (for the pair above)

4 head pins or dangle pins, 2 inches (5 cm) in length

2 double hangers

6 jump rings, 3mm in size

2 ear wires

Clear gloss spray enamel or varnish (optional)

Tools

Craft drill with a ¹⁄₁₆-inch (.16-cm) drill bit

Wire cutters

Round-nose pliers

Flat-nose pliers

Instructions

One
Drill holes in the gingko and Kentucky coffee tree seeds. Drill each lengthwise, from end to end.

Two
Thread the beads and seeds on the head pins or dangle pins as shown. Using the wire cutters, trim approximately ¼ to ½ inch (.5 to 1.5 cm) off the tops of one pair of head pins holding either the Kentucky coffee seed or the gingko seeds. (This will allow one seed to hang shorter than the other on each earring.)

Three
Use the round-nose pliers to make a loop at the top of each of the four beaded head pins. Using the flat-nose pliers, attach the loops of the head pins to the double hangers with jump rings.

Four
Attach the ear wires to the tops of the double hangers with jump rings.

Five
If desired, finish with several coats of clear spray enamel or varnish. To avoid drips, apply light coats, allowing each coat to dry before applying the next one.

CHRISTMAS SPICE NECKLACE

You get an added bonus when you make this neck-lace! The delightful aroma of these spices creates a festive potpourri that evokes memories of the holiday season. To keep the scent fresh and strong, store the necklace in a self-sealing plastic bag between each wearing.

Materials

40 pieces of cinnamon sticks, each approximately ¾ inch (2 cm) long

40 whole allspice berries

1 whole star anise

Beading thread

82 round gold beads, 2mm in diameter (optional)

Red wood bead, 3mm in diameter

24-gauge brass wire, 15 inches (38 cm)

1 jump ring, 3mm in size

Craft glue

Tools

Small saw (optional)

Craft drill with a #61 bit

Scissors

Beading needle that can pass through the small drilled holes

Round-nose pliers

2 pairs of flat-nose pliers, one with smooth jaws, one with serrated jaws

Wire cutters

Instructions

One

Break or saw twigs of curled cinnamon sticks into 40 pieces that are each approximately ¾ inch (2 cm) long. Using the craft drill and #61 drill bit, drill holes through the pieces of the cinnamon sticks crosswise at the center point of their length.

Two

Drill through the whole allspice lengthwise.

Three

Thread the needle with the beading thread. String the cinnamon twigs, allspice, and beads (optional) as shown, making the necklace long enough to slip over your head. Tie the ends of the beading thread in a knot. You may want to apply a drop of craft glue to the knot to secure it.

Four

To prepare the star anise, first choose a perfect star with unbroken points. Take the wire and center it across the star, so that each end of the wire is of equal length. Working diagonally through each interval between star spokes, wrap the wire around from the front to the back, then from the back to front. The detail photograph below shows you how the wire should look on the back and front of the star when finished.

Back

Front

Five

When you've finished wrapping the wire, twist both free ends together into an upright "ponytail." Onto this tail, using both ends of wire as one, string a gold bead, the red wooden bead, and another gold bead.

Six

Use the round-nose pliers to make a loop approximately ⅜ inch (1 cm) from the top of the last gold bead. Holding the loop with the smooth-jaw flat-nose pliers, use the serrated-jaw flat-nose pliers to twist the ends of the wire around the shaft of the tail. Trim any excess wire with wire cutters. If necessary, take up any slack in the wire around the star anise by gently twisting the wire on the back with pliers. Be careful—if you twist too much or use too much pressure, the star anise may break.

Seven

Attach a jump ring to the loop you just made, using the jump ring to attach the star anise medallion to the middle of the necklace.

Variation: Add whole cloves to the necklace for added aroma. Use the craft drill and small drill bit to carefully drill the cloves crosswise, just under the bud on the stem. You may need to buy more cloves than you think you'll need, since some of them will break when drilled.

Nutmeg and Allspice Necklace

For an interesting woodlike bead, try using slices of whole nutmeg. When cut crosswise, the nutmeg shows a subtle and intricate grain pattern that looks almost hand-painted. You'll also be able to enjoy the aroma of the nutmeg every time you wear this necklace.

Materials

12 or so medium-sized whole nutmegs, enough to make approximately 19 slices, each 3/16 inch (.4 cm) thick

18 whole allspice berries

Tigertail

37 round gold beads, 3mm in diameter

2 crimp beads

3 jump rings, 3mm in size

Gold chain, 3-inch (7.5-cm) length

1 jump ring, 4mm in size

Gold clasp

Tools

Dust mask

Vise

Craft drill with cutoff wheels and mandrel to fit

Craft knife with a sharp blade

#400 sandpaper

2 drill bits for the craft drill, one 1/32 inch (.08 cm), one 1/16 inch (.16 cm)

Crimping pliers

Flat-nose pliers

Wire cutters

Instructions

Wear a dust mask when slicing, drilling, or sanding nutmeg. Though not poisonous in small amounts, you want to avoid inhaling excessive amounts when working.

One

Place a whole nutmeg horizontally in the jaws of the vise, leaving approximately half of the nutmeg free. With the craft drill and cutoff wheel on the mandrel, cut off the "heel" end of the nutmeg. Then continue cutting slices, each 3/16 inch (.4 cm) thick. You'll get approximately two slices per half of nutmeg. Turn the nutmeg around in the vise, so that the vise is gripping only a little bit of the sliced-off end. With the cutoff wheel, slice off the other heel and make one or two more slices. Repeat with the rest of the nutmegs until you have 19 slices (plus a few more for practice). If necessary, use a craft knife with a sharp blade to trim off the brown color on the face of each slice so that the intricate pattern is visible. Sand and shape the edges of each slice, if desired.

Two

Using the craft drill with the small 1/32-inch (.08-cm) drill bit, drill through each nutmeg slice, from edge to edge, centering the hole as best you can.

Three

Using the craft drill with the 1/16-inch (.16-cm) drill bit, drill holes through the whole allspice seeds.

Four

Using the photograph as a guide, string the seeds, nutmeg slices, and gold beads onto the tigertail. When finished, leave a long end of tigertail at each end of the strung beads. Thread one end of the tigertail through a crimp bead, then thread the end back through the crimp bead and into several of the beads on the necklace. Pull up any slack in the tigertail to make a small loop above the crimp bead. With the crimping pliers, crush the crimp bead to secure the tigertail, then trim any excess wire with the wire cutters. Use the flat-nose pliers to attach a 3mm jump ring to the loop. Repeat for the other end of the necklace.

Five

Use the wire cutters to cut the length of chain into two pieces. At one end of one piece of chain, attach a 3mm jump ring. At one end of the other piece, attach the 4mm jump ring. Attach the other ends of the chain to the two jump rings on the ends of the tigertail loops. Then attach the clasp to the end of the chain that has the 3mm jump ring on it.

Tip: Keep this necklace in an airtight plastic bag between wearings to retain the wonderful nutmeg aroma.

Eucalyptus Necklace and Earrings

When you hear the word euca-lyptus, you might immediately think of the fragrant leaves used in floral arrangements and wreaths. The woody seed pods used in this project, however, come from the blue gum eucalyptus.

Materials

Necklace

9 blue gum eucalyptus seed pods

9 head pins, 2 inches (5 cm) in length

45 silver beads of various shapes and sizes

13 jump rings, 4mm in size

Dark brown leather cord, 60 inches (1.5 m) long

5 ostrich eggshell beads (pur-chased), or any flat, round beads approximately ½ inch (1.5 cm) wide by ⅛ inch (.3 cm) thick

6 fold-over crimp ends, large enough to fit the cord

6 jump rings, 3mm in size

2 bead separators with three holes

Chain, 6-inch (15-cm) length

1 toggle-and-loop clasp

Earrings

- 2 blue gum eucalyptus seed pods
- 2 head pins, 2 inches (5 cm) in length
- 14 silver beads of different textures and sizes
- 2 jump rings, 3mm in size
- 2 ear wires

Tools

- Craft drill with a ¹⁄₁₆-inch (.16-cm) drill bit
- Wire cutters
- Round-nose pliers
- Flat-nose pliers
- Scissors
- Needle-nose pliers with serrated jaws

Instructions

Necklace

One

Using the craft drill with the ¹⁄₁₆-inch (.16-cm) drill bit, drill holes lengthwise through the eucalyptus seed pods.

Two

Thread three or more silver beads onto a head pin, then insert the head pin through the seed pod. Place two or more beads on top of the seed pod. With the wire cutters, trim the head pin to approximately ¼ inch (.5 cm) above the top of the last bead. Using the round-nose pliers, make a loop in the free end of the head pin. Using the flat-nose pliers, attach a 4mm jump ring to the loop. This is one seed-pod set. Repeat for the remaining eight eucalyptus pods.

Three

Cut the leather cord into three pieces, making one piece 18 inches (45.5 cm) long, one piece 20 inches (51 cm) long, and one piece 22 inches (56 cm) long.

Four

With the longest piece of leather cord, tie an overhand knot approximately 3 inches (5 cm) from one end. String on a seed-pod set. Tie another overhand knot close to the seed-pod set. Repeat stringing the pods and tying the knots as above with four more seed-pod sets. Try to space the pod sets approximately 2¼ to 2½ inches (5.5-6.5 cm) apart. As desired, randomly string on a few beads of your choice, including the flat, round ostrich eggshell beads.

Five

With the 20-inch (51-cm) length of leather cord, repeat the overhand knot and stringing sequence as in Step 3 with three seed-pod sets. Place the first seed-pod set approximately 5 inches (12.5 cm) from the end of the cord.

Six

With the shortest piece of leather cord, string on the last seed-pod set, placing it in the middle of the length of cord. Make overhand knots on both sides of the seed-pod set.

Seven

Using the needle-nose pliers, attach a fold-over crimp end to each of the six ends of the leather cord, then attach a 3mm jump ring to each of the loops on the crimp ends.

Eight

With the jump rings, attach one end of each of the three lengths of cord to one of the three holes in one separator, then attach the other three ends to the corresponding holes in the other separator. Make sure that the three leather cords remain parallel and untangled when connecting the ends to the separators.

Nine

Cut the 6-inch (15-cm) length of chain into two 3-inch (7.5- cm) lengths. Attach a 4mm jump ring to each of the ends of the chain. Attach one end of each of the two pieces of chain to the two separators. Attach the other ends of the chain pieces to the two sections of the toggle-and-loop clasp.

Earrings

One

Following the necklace directions for drilling the eucalyptus pods, drill holes lengthwise in two seed pods.

Two

On one 2-inch (5-cm) head pin, place three beads, a seed pod, and three or four more beads. With the wire cutters, trim the head pin to approximately ¼ inch (.5 cm) above the top of the last bead.

Three

Using the round-nose pliers, make a loop in the free end of the head pin. Using the flat-nose pliers, attach a 3mm jump ring to the loop. Attach an ear wire to the jump ring. Repeat for the other earring.

Job's Tears and Mary's Bean Rosary

Mary's bean, of all the drift seeds, travels the farthest on the ocean currents. By wrapping wire around it, I was able to highlight its natural indentations which are in the shape of a cross. The pearly gray seeds, Job's Tears, were named for Job of the Old Testamont.

Materials

59 head pins, 2 inches (5 cm) long

59 Job's tears

Chain, 13-inch (33-cm) length

26 jump rings, 4mm in size

1 Mary's bean

1 piece of 18- to 24-gauge wire, 6 inches (15 cm) in length

Tools

Wire cutters

Round-nose pliers

2 pairs of flat-nose pliers, one with smooth jaws and one with serrated jaws

Instructions

This rosary, like all traditional Catholic rosaries, is composed of five decades of beads (groups of 10) for counting Ave Maria prayers; six single beads for counting the Our Father prayers; three additional beads for counting Ave Maria prayers; and a crucifix.

One

Using the wire cutters, cut off the heads on the head pins. On one end of one of these pins, use the round-nose pliers to make a loop. Using the smooth-jaw flat-nose pliers to hold the loop, use the serrated-jaw flat-nose pliers to wrap the end of the wire around the shaft of the pin. Trim any excess wire with the wire cutters. Put a Job's tear lengthwise on the head pin. (You do not need to drill the seeds beforehand.) As above, make a loop on the other end of the head pin.

Two

Push another head pin through a second Job's tear. Using the round-nose pliers, make a loop on one end. Do not wrap the end of the wire around the shaft yet.

Three

Take the loop made in Step 2 and attach it to one of the loops of the first bead, making sure both beads face the same way. Using both pairs of flat-nose pliers as before, hold the new loop with one pair while wrapping the end around the shaft with the other. Trim any excess wire. Following the same procedure, make a loop and wrap the wire on the remaining end of the head pin.

Four

Repeat Steps 2 and 3 for each of eight more beads until you have a series of 10 beads on head pins.

Five

Using the wire cutters, cut a ¾-inch (2-cm) length of chain. Count the links in this section. When cutting each piece of chain for use between decades you won't need to measure, just count the links.

Six

Attach one 4mm jump ring to the end loop on the last bead in a series of 10, then attach one end of a cut piece of chain.

Seven

Following the photograph as your guide, continue connecting looped head pins, jump rings, and sections of chain. Between decades you will have a jump ring, a length of chain, a jump ring, a single bead, a jump ring, a length of chain, and a jump ring that will be attached to the loop of the first bead of the next decade. Make five decades.

Eight

When you complete the loop on the last bead of the fifth decade, attach a jump ring to it, then attach one end of a 1½-inch (4-cm) length of chain to the jump ring. Complete the circle by attaching a jump ring to the other end of the chain, and attaching the jump ring to the loop on the first bead of the first decade.

NINE

Following the procedures above for connecting wired beads to the chain with jump rings, make a straight length in this pattern: chain; a single bead; chain; three beads; chain; and a single bead.

TEN

Prepare the Mary's bean. First, if necessary, clean and polish the bean (see page 35). With the 6-inch (15-cm) piece of wire, wrap the bean as you would wrap a box, making the cross at the back of the bean and leaving just a tiny bit of slack in the wire. Twist the wires to secure, then cut the ends of the wire, tucking the ends under the twist. Flatten the twist to the bean's back surface.

ELEVEN

So that the bean will hang straight, attach a jump ring to the wire at the top of the Mary's bean. After closing the jump ring, give the wires on the back of the Mary's bean a quarter twist to take up any slack in the wire.

TWELEVE

Attach the bean to the chain on the straight length of chain and beads. Using a jump ring, attach the last single bead on the straight length of beads and chain to the center link of the 1½-inch (4-cm) length of chain on the circle of beads.

Sea Bean and Nickernut Bracelet

If you live far from the ocean, enlist the help of others in procuring your drift seeds. Whether your family or friends live at the shore or are just occasional beach bums, you can share your knowledge of drift seeds with them, while giving them a good excuse to take a walk on the beach.

Materials

- 4 nickernuts
- 3 sea beans
- Tigertail
- 2 silver crimp beads
- 4 flat silver spacer beads, approximately ¼ inch (.5 cm) in diameter
- 8 disk-shaped bone beads (purchased)
- Silver clasp
- 2 silver jump rings, 4mm in diameter

Tools

- Craft drill with a ⅟16-inch (.16-cm) drill bit
- Wire cutters
- Crimping pliers

Instructions

One
Using the craft drill with the ⅟16-inch (.16-cm) drill bit, drill lengthwise holes in the sea beans and the nickernuts.

Two
Using the wire cutters, cut a 15-inch (38-cm) length of tigertail. Thread one end of the tigertail through a crimp bead, then thread the end of the tigertail back through the same crimp bead, leaving a small loop in the tigertail above the crimp bead. To secure, use the crimping pliers to crush the crimp bead.

Three
Using the photograph as your guide, string the beads and seeds on the tigertail as follows: two silver spacer beads; a bone bead; the sea beans and nickernuts, alternating between the two, and placing a bone bead between them; two silver spacer beads.

Four
String the second crimp bead on the end of the tigertail, then back through the same crimp bead. Pull up any slack, leaving a small loop of tigertail above the crimp bead. To secure, use the crimping pliers to crush the crimp bead.

Five
To finish, attach the clasp to the tigertail loops with the jump rings.

Seeded Watch

For an unusual timepiece, use seeds and beads to create a novel watchband. Watch beadbars, found in bead shops, are made to accommodate a watch face, allowing you to quickly fashion this project.

Materials

Pairs of matching seeds and gold beads (the number will depend on wrist size)

Watch face

2 watch beadbars

Clasp

Tigertail

12 crimp beads

Tools

Craft drill with a ⅟₁₆-inch (.16-cm) drill bit (or smaller)

Tape measure

Watch tool (for removing the pins on the watch)

Crimping pliers

Wire cutters

Instructions

One
Using the craft drill and the ⅟₁₆-inch (.16-cm), or smaller, drill bit, drill holes in the seeds lengthwise.

Two
Determine the wrist size by using a tape measure to measure the wrist, or use an average wrist size; the average wrist size for women is 7 inches (18 cm). Add 1 inch (2.5 cm) to this measurement for comfort, giving you the total wrist size that you'll be working with.

Three
Using the watch tool on the pins of the watch, attach the beadbars to both sides of the watch face.

Four
To get the measurement needed for cutting the tigertail lengths, follow this sequence:
a) Measure the watch face and attached beadbars.
b) Measure the length of both the clasp pieces with the clasp closed.
c) Add the measurements of step a and step b together.
d) Subtract this sum from the total wrist size determined in Step 2.
e) Add approximately ½ inch (1.5 cm) to this sum.

Five
Cut as many tigertail lengths to the measurement determined in Step 3 as are needed to accommodate the holes in your watch beadbars. (The ones shown here have three holes, therefore I cut six lengths.)

Six
Thread a crimp bead onto the end of one of the tigertail lengths. Thread the end of the tigertail into one of the holes of the watch beadbar that is attached to the watch face. Loop the end of the tigertail over the beadbar and back into the crimp bead. Using the crimping pliers, crush the crimp bead, securing the end of the tigertail. Trim any excess tigertail using wire cutters. Repeat for each length of tigertail, attaching them to both sides of the watch face.

Seven
String the beads and seeds in your desired design. Following Step 4 for looping the tigertail and using crimp beads, attach the ends of the beaded tigertail to the clasp pieces.

CANNA AND DRIFTWOOD ROSARY

Canna seeds, with their oval shape and smooth shells, provide a tactile complement to these prayer beads.

They are naturally a matte black, but can be polished to a shine using a jeweler's cloth. The driftwood cross and "medal" are easy to make, or purchase a cross and medal to incorporate into your design.

Materials

- 58 canna seeds
- Small pieces of driftwood
- Beading thread
- Tigertail, 12 inches (30.5 cm)
- 89 silver beads, 3mm in diameter
- 4 silver crimp beads
- Craft glue
- Sandpaper
- Furniture oil

Tools

- Needle to fit beading thread
- Scissors
- Black felt-tipped pen
- Craft knife or whittling knife
- Sandpaper or sanding drum for a craft drill
- Craft drill and 1/16-inch (.16-cm) drill bit
- Vise
- Electric drill with a 1/2-inch-round (1.5 cm) plug cutter
- Crimping pliers

Instructions

One

To make the main circle of beads, tie several overlapping, overhand knots at one end of the beading thread. Thread the needle with the other end of the thread. Using the photo as your guide, string the silver beads and canna seeds.

Two

When the circle is complete, pull up any slack from the knotted end of the thread, then tie the two ends of the thread together using several square knots. Thread the ends of the thread onto the needle, and pass the needle and thread back through the seeds and beads to conceal the ends of the thread. Cut off any excess thread. Apply a drop of craft glue to the knot and let dry.

Three

To make the cross, use the pen to draw the cross shape on the driftwood. Use a craft or whittling knife to carve the cross. Sandpaper by hand, or use the sanding drum on a craft drill to sand the cross smooth. Drill a hole in the top of the cross using a 1/16-inch (.16-cm) drill bit on a craft drill. Saturate the cross and medal with furniture oil to keep the wood from drying out.

Four

To make the medal, use an electric drill and 1/2-inch-round (1.5-cm) plug cutter to cut out the round shape. Hold the wood in the vise for cutting the plug. You can also carve the medal out of wood using a craft or whittling knife. After the medal is cut or carved, sand it smooth. With the craft drill and a 1/16-inch (.16-cm) drill bit, drill two opposite holes in the medal. Saturate the medal with furniture oil.

Five

To finish the rosary, take a 6-inch (15-cm) length of tigertail and thread one end through one crimp bead. Loop the end of the tigertail around the beading thread at the space in the middle of the six-bead series of silver beads on the original circle. Thread the tigertail back through the crimp bead, pull it up tight, and crush the crimp bead with the crimping pliers. Leave approximately a 1/2-inch (2.5-cm) end of wire free.

Six

Thread three silver beads onto the wire end. Thread the free end of the wire through a crimp bead, then through one hole in the medal, then back through the crimp bead (concealing the wire end through beads). Pull the wire tight and crush the crimp bead with the crimping pliers. Trim any excess wire.

Seven

Using 6 inches (15 cm) of tigertail, thread one end through a crimp bead, then through the other hole in the medal, then back through the crimp bead. Pull the wire up tight, and crush the crimp bead with the crimping pliers.

Eight

On this length of tigertail, string the beads and seeds as shown in the photograph, then thread the tigertail through the hole in the cross, then back through the crimp bead. Pull the wire end tight, stringing it back through the beads to conceal the end. Crush the crimp bead with crimping pliers. Trim any excess wire.

Hair Sticks of African Porcupine Quills and Assorted Baubles

Have fun gathering the baubles for decorating the ends of these hair sticks; attaching them with chain adds an extra element of movement to this design. Regrettably, I did not travel to Africa to obtain these quills; they were a purchase I couldn't resist. They are very sharp, so use caution when handling them before you trim the ends.

Materials

3 African porcupine quills

3 jump rings, 8mm in size

Small jump rings, 3mm in size

Chain

Wire

Head pins

Miscellaneous seeds, shells, beads, etc., used here: coconut shell pieces; mescal bean; cowrie shell (purchased); snail seashell; bead made from cattle horn; sea coconut slice; lucky nut seed (yellow oleander) (purchased); bottle glass shard; candlenut seed (purchased);large silver bead; and small metal beads

Tools

Wire cutters or scissors

Craft drill with a ⅟16-inch (.16-cm) drill bit

Sandpaper, coarse grit (#60-#100), or emery board

Round-nose pliers

Flat-nose pliers

Instructions

One

Using the wire cutters or scissors, clip off the sharp ends of each quill. Sand the top (the non-sharp end that attaches to the porcupine) smooth using the sandpaper or an emery board.

Two

Use the craft drill with the ⅟16-inch (.16-cm) drill bit to drill a hole through the top of each quill, approximately ¼ inch (.5 cm) from the end. Place an 8mm jump ring through each hole.

Three

Drill holes in selected beads, seeds, shells, etc., as necessary. Following the photograph as your guide, make the baubles by using head pins, chain, beads, and jump rings to assemble the components in designs of your choice. Use the round-nose pliers to make loops as necessary and flat-nose pliers to help you twist wire when needed. Attach the baubles to the 8mm jump rings at the top of the quill using the smaller jump rings. Each of these hair sticks has three baubles attached to it.

10-Bean Soup Necklace

A quick trip to the supermarket will yield most of the materials you'll need to make this necklace. You can buy a pre-packaged, dried-bean soup mix. Or, spend time in a store that specializes in selling bulk items to see what manner of exotic seeds and beans you can find.

MATERIALS

Mixed dried beans, 4 ounces (112 g)—a 10-bean soup mix is ideal*

68 soybeans

15-20 squash seeds

Acorns

Tamarind seeds

Calico beans (red and white)

Twig sections

Bamboo sections (optional)

8-10 round beads, 3mm in diameter

Tigertail

Tools

Hobby drill with a 1/16-inch (.16-cm), or smaller, drill bit

Scissors

*Ten-bean soup mix generally includes black beans, black-eyed peas, great Northern beans, small red beans, large and small lima beans, pinto beans, yellow and green split peas, and pink beans.

INSTRUCTIONS

ONE
Drill holes in the beans, seeds, acorns, twigs, and tamarind seeds. Cut a few bamboo slices to use (optional).

TWO
Randomly string the materials on the tigertail. This design places a soy bean between each seed.

THREE
Tie the ends of the tigertail, or use a crimp end to secure. To hide the ends, string them back into the beads, and cut off any excess.

MATTERS OF COMPOST

If you're a gardener, you know the value of compost and the ease of making it. Since you're collecting and using organic materials, save the scraps from drilling and cutting for your compost bin. At your workbench, use a whisk broom to sweep up all leftover organic bits and pieces, including plant "saw-dust," parts of seeds, pods, twig scraps, bone, and broken seashells, into a small lidded garbage can. When the container is full, simply toss all the debris into your compost bin.

Fish-Jaw Necklace

While beachcombing, I was attracted by this fish jaw's bleached white color and weathered texture. Because the bone threatened to break apart at its natural suture (seam) line between bony plates, I knew I needed to devise some way to protect my find.

By drilling small holes through the bone, lacing wire through each hole, and twisting the wire ends tight on the back of the bone, my surgical reinforcement became a handsome decorative motif. I liked the look so much that I used the same technique on a weak place on the upper right horn of the bone.

You can adapt this technique on any bone or piece of wood that you might find, even if it doesn't need reinforcing. Before you begin drilling, you might find it helpful to make a few sketches of possible designs for lacing the wire.

MATERIALS

16 soapberry seeds

1 twig, approximately ½ inch (1.5 cm) in diameter and 1 to 2 inches (2.5-5 cm) long

1 piece of cork, driftwood, or bone, approximately ¾ x 1¼ inches (2 x 3 cm), and ¾ inch (2 cm) thick—thick enough to divide into two pieces

4 gold jump rings, 6mm in size

1 fish jaw (substitute any v-shaped piece of bone or wood, or carve your own from bone or wood)

4 gold jump rings, 4mm in size

Brass wire, 22- or 24-gauge

1 corn husk or felt scrap

Craft glue

Fine gold chain with clasp

6 gold jump rings, 3 mm in size

1 yard (.9 m) of tigertail

20 round gold beads, 3mm in diameter

4 gold crimp beads

Tools

Craft drill with a 1/16-inch (.16-cm) drill bit, and a #61 bit for making the holes for the wire.

Small saw with a fine-tooth blade, or saw attachment for your craft drill

Scissors

Flat-nose pliers

Wire cutters

Round-nose pliers

Crimping pliers

INSTRUCTIONS

ONE

Using the craft drill and the 1/16-inch (.16-cm) drill bit, drill the soapberry seeds lengthwise.

TWO

Using the saw or saw attachment for your craft drill, saw lengthwise through the center of the twig. In the same way, saw the cork through its thickness to make two somewhat matching pieces. Drill a hole through the center of the cork sections. Drill holes at each end of the two twig sections. Using the flat-nose piers, attach the 6mm jump rings to both ends of each twig piece.

THREE

To accommodate the chain for hanging the bone pendant, use the smaller drill bit to drill two holes in the bone, one on each side of the v-shape. Attach a 4mm jump ring to each hole.

FOUR

To decorate the bone with wire, use the smaller drill bit to drill parallel holes on either side of the suture line, or according to your design. If the wire is just for decoration and not for repair, you may want to use a single piece of wire and lace it continuously through the holes. For reinforcement of weak bone or flaws in other materials, I prefer to cut the wire into short pieces, which I lace separately through two parallel holes, twisting the ends in back to secure. To prevent any exposed wires from catching on clothing, glue a piece of corn husk or felt over the wires.

FIVE

Using the wire cutters, cut the chain approximately 1½ inches (4 cm) away from each clasp end, creating two sections of chain with a piece of the clasp on either end. Attach a 3mm jump ring to the free ends of each chain. Set the remaining chain aside.

SIX

Cut two pieces of tigertail, each about a foot (30.5 cm) long.

Using the round-nose pliers, make a loop at one end of a tigertail piece. Attach a crimp end to the bottom of the loop, then use the crimping pliers to close the crimp end and secure the loop. String the beads, seeds, and cork on the tigertail, as shown. Finish the section by pulling the tigertail tight against the beads, making a loop with the round-nose pliers, and securing it using the crimping pliers and crimp end. Cut away any excess tigertail. Attach a 3mm jump ring to this end loop. Repeat to make the beaded section for the other side.

SEVEN

To assemble the necklace, attach the loop of the beaded section without the jump ring to the jump ring at the end of one of the chain pieces cut in Step 5. At the other end, attach the 3mm jump ring on the Tigertail loop to the 6mm jump ring on one end of the twig. Repeat for the other side.

EIGHT

Cut two chain sections from the remaining chain from Step 5. The length of the chain sections will depend on the length of necklace desired. Adjust the length of chain until the pendant drapes as you wish, then cut the chain accordingly. On one end of each chain attach a 3mm jump ring, on the other end of each chain attach a 4mm jump ring.

NINE

Attach the end of the chain with the 4mm jump ring to the 6mm jump ring on the end of the twig section, then attach the end of the chain with the 3mm jump ring to the 4mm jump ring on the bone pendant. Repeat for the other side.

Mini-Gourd Necklace and Gourd Earrings

Dyan Peterson, a nationally known gourd artist and teacher, made this pendant and earrings from her favorite raw material. Because gourds provide a natural blank canvas, you can embellish them any way you want. They take dye easily, and are interesting when engraved or decorated using a wood-burning tool.

Materials

Pendant

1 Japanese mini-gourd—available at farmers' markets, through gourd-supply catalogues, or grow your own!

Leather dye in brown, turquoise, and British tan—available at shoe repair shops, at craft shops, or through leather-supply companies.

Clear satin-finish spray lacquer

Black cord in silk or cotton

Assorted small beads for stringing

Earrings

Gourd of any size

Leather dye in British tan, black, and red

Clear satin-finish spray lacquer

Metallic gold pen

2 small sticks

2 Beads

Quick-drying glue

2 earring posts with 10mm pads, or 2 ear wires with 2 jump rings

Tools

Stiff scrub brush

Grapefruit spoon--or any spoon with a serrated tip

Craft saw with fine-tooth saw blades

Pencil

Paper or cardboard for template

Tape

Wood-burning tool with small straight tip

Paper plate

6 foam brushes, 1 inch (2.5 cm) wide

Craft tool with a small engraving attachment or hand engraving tool

Hand drill or awl

Fine sandpaper (#400-#600)

Instructions

Pendant

One

If the outside of the gourd is dirty, use warm water and a stiff brush to remove the dirt and mold. Be careful not to scratch the surface. Allow the gourd to dry completely.

Two

Turn the mini-gourd on its side and very carefully cut the top off using the craft saw and fine-tooth blades. When you have cut three-fourths of the way through the top, cut very slowly the rest of the way to avoid cracking the gourd.

Three

With the pencil, draw three abstract squares around the top fourth of the gourd. Using the wood-burning tool, trace over the pencil lines. Do not burn too deeply, otherwise you may go right through the gourd.

Four

To cut down on the mess when using dyes, use paper plates as disposable palettes. Using one of the foam brushes, paint the top part of the gourd with the brown leather dye. Allow the dye to dry. Next, using another foam brush, paint the inside of the square with the turquoise leather dye and allow to dry. With a third foam brush, paint the rest of the gourd with the British tan leather dye. Allow the dye to dry.

Five

Spray on the clear satin-finish lacquer. To avoid drips, apply several light coats rather than one heavy coat, allowing each coat to dry

completely before applying the next one. Allow the lacquer to dry.

SIX

Draw four abstract shapes inside the corners of the square, then using the carving tool, carve out the abstract shapes.

SEVEN

Make holes on either side of the top of the gourd with the awl or hand drill. If you are working with a thin-walled gourd, do this carefully to avoid cracking the gourd.

EIGHT

Cut the cord to the desired length. String a few groupings of beads on the cord, holding them in place with small knots. Thread the ends of the cord into the holes in the gourd, securing each end with a knot on the inside of the gourd.

ONE

If the outside of the gourd is dirty, use warm water and a stiff brush to remove the dirt and mold. Be careful not to scratch the surface.

TWO

Use an awl or a drill to pierce a hole in the gourd that's big enough for the saw blade. Insert the saw blade, and cut the gourd in half in any direction. Then cut the halves again, cutting the gourd into quarters. Use a grapefruit spoon to clean out the inside of the gourd.

THREE

Make a template from paper or cardboard of the desired shape you want for your earring and cut it out. Tape the template onto the gourd surface and trace around the pattern with a pencil.

FOUR

Using the handsaw, cut out two matching shapes. Clean the backs of the shapes, then sand the backs, fronts, and sides lightly with fine sandpaper (#400-#600).

FIVE

Using a pencil, draw two horizontal straight lines ⅔ of the way down from the top of the earring, spacing them approximately ¼ inch (.5 cm) apart. With a wood-burning tool, trace over the pencil lines.

SIX

To cut down on the mess when using dyes, use paper plates as disposable palettes. Using a disposable foam brush, paint the top portion of the earring with the British tan leather dye. Using another brush, paint the area between the lines with red leather dye. If you find this color too bright, add a little British tan dye to tone down the color to a more subtle and earthy hue. Using the third brush, apply black leather dye to the bottom portion of the earrings. Let dry.

SEVEN

Draw small abstract shapes onto the bottom black portion of the earring. Using the craft tool with engraving attachment, carve the shapes. You can also do this using a small hand-carving tool or knife. Using the metallic gold pen, trace the carvings. Let dry.

EIGHT

Seal the earrings with clear satin-finish spray lacquer. Apply three (or more) coats, allowing each coat to dry thoroughly before applying the next coat. Be careful not to spray too much lacquer in any one coat; it will run and create drips. The more coats you apply, the shinier your earrings will be.

NINE

Apply black leather dye to coat the back and sides of the earrings. Be careful not to apply too much dye to the sides and back because it will absorb and soak into the carvings on the front side. (If the gourd is thin, you may want to use black spray paint instead of the dye.)

TEN

Thread a small stick through a large bead. Glue the bead to the red area between the two horizontal lines. You may need to put a small amount of glue in the hole to hold the stick in place.

ELEVEN

Glue the 10mm pad to the back of the earring. The larger pad will give you a larger gluing surface. If you want to use ear wires, use the awl to make small holes at the tops of your earrings then attach the wires with jump rings.

Pawpaw Bracelet

The design of this bracelet lends it a quiet elegance. You'll be surprised how simple it is to make. The large pawpaw seeds quickly cover the distance around the beading wire, while the flat silver beads provide a harmonious grace note to the natural materials.

Materials

7 pawpaw seeds

Tigertail

2 silver crimp beads

1 silver toggle and clasp set

2 melon-shaped silver beads, ⅜ inch (1 cm in diameter)

2 silver beads, 4mm in diameter

Flat silver spacer beads, 7mm in diameter

Tools

Craft drill with a ½₂-inch (.08-cm) drill bit

Wire cutters

Crimping pliers

Instructions

One

Using the craft drill with the ½₂-inch (.08-cm) drill bit, drill holes lengthwise in the pawpaw seeds.

Two

Cut a length of tigertail, approximately 10 inches (25.5 cm) long. Place a crimp bead on one end of the tigertail. Loop the end of the tigertail around one side of the clasp set, then loop the tigertail back through the crimp bead. Using the crimping pliers, crush the crimp bead to secure the tigertail.

Three

String the following on the tigertail: one 4mm silver bead; one melon-shaped bead; one pawpaw seed; and one silver spacer bead. String on the remaining pawpaw seeds and spacer beads. Finish with a melon-shaped bead, a 4mm silver bead, and a crimp bead. Loop the tigertail around the other end of the clasp set, then loop the tigertail back through the crimp bead. Using the crimping pliers, crush the crimp bead to secure the tigertail.

Four

Trim the ends of the tigertail with wire cutters.

Black Walnut Earrings, Bracelet and Belt

If you live in an area where black walnuts grow, you can gather the materials for these fashion accessories in no time. The sliced nut shells naturally provide convenient holes for weaving the leather strips. As a bonus, you'll be able to enjoy the tasty meat of this nut while you work. Judy Mallow, an artist in pine needle basketry, designed these pieces.

Materials

Black walnuts

Shellac or clear acrylic spray

Leather or suede strips, ³⁄₁₆ inch (.4 cm) wide

Quick-drying glue

2 ear wires

2 jump rings, 3mm

Tools

Band saw, coping saw, or fine-tooth handsaw

Vise

Nut picks or craft knife

Fine sandpaper #200–#400

Craft drill or power drill with ¹⁄₁₆-inch (.16 cm) bit

Tape measure

Scissors

Instructions

One

Using the saw, cut the nuts to get slices that are ¼ inch (.5 cm) wide (or less). For the earrings, cut two slices. The number of slices you will need for the bracelet and belt depends on the measurement of the wrist and waist you are outfitting.

Two

Clean the nut meat from the slices using the nut picks or craft knife. Sand both sides of the nut slices.

Three

For the earrings, use a craft drill or power drill with a ¹⁄₁₆-inch (.16-cm) drill bit to drill a hole at the top edge of each nut slice.

Four

For the earrings, bracelet, and belt, use the shellac or clear acrylic spray to coat both sides of the nut slices. Let them dry.

Five

To finish the earrings, attach the ear wires to the nut slices with jump rings.

Six

For the bracelet, lay the nut slices you are using end to end, then measure this length. Since you will be weaving one strip of leather through one side of the slices, then through the other side, cut one strip of leather that is double the measurement of the end-to-end slices plus 6 inches (15 cm). The extra 6 inches (15 cm) will provide some slack, plus make the loop that will wrap around a nut slice to close the bracelet.

Seven

Glue one end of the leather strip to the back of the first nut slice. Weave the leather through one side of the slices, then through the other, leaving a loop at the end of the length of slices that is large enough to go around the first slice. Adjust the slack on the leather; you want to leave enough room for the bracelet to circle the wrist comfortably. To finish, trim any extra leather, then glue the free end of the leather strip to the back of the first nut as you did when you began weaving.

Eight

For the belt, cut two strips of leather that are each long enough to go around the waist, adding extra length to the strips for the ends that will drape after tying the belt. Weave two parallel strips of leather through the nut slices. Using two overhand knots or a square knot, tie the ends of the two parallel strips together at both ends of the length of slices to hold the slices in place. If desired, you can string a few beads on the very end of the strips, securing the beads with knots.

Green Pea and Pumpkin Seed Necklace

This is a necklace you can very well grow in your own garden. If you don't have the space, or a green thumb, a quick trip to the grocery store will provide you with all natural raw materials you'll need. The delicate coloration of the green peas, sprayed with clear enamel to make them glossy, makes the beads look like pale jade—belying the fact that they are merely humble legumes.

Materials

69 dried green peas

69 pumpkin seeds

Clear high-gloss spray enamel or lacquer

Beading thread

Craft glue

Tools

Craft drill with a 1⁄16-inch (.16-cm), or smaller, drill bit

Scissors

Sewing needle to fit beading thread

Instructions

One
Using the craft drill and the 1⁄16-inch (.16-cm), or smaller, drill bit, drill holes in the green peas.

Two
Cut a 30-inch (76-cm) length of beading thread, and thread the needle onto one end.

Three
Using the photograph as your guide, string the green peas and pumpkin seeds onto the string. This necklace alternates three green peas with three pumpkin seeds. The pumpkin seeds can be pierced with the sewing needle as you go.

Four
To finish, tie the ends of the beading thread together with several overhand or square knots. Trim the thread ends, then place a dot of craft glue on the knots for security.

Five
Spray the green peas with clear high-gloss enamel or varnish and allow to dry thoroughly.

Kentucky Coffee Tree, Gingko Seed and Cycad Necklace

The central seed for this necklace comes from the cycad plant (Cycas revoluta). With its single trunk topped with multiple dark green leaves, this ancient plant is often mistaken for a palm tree. If you can't find a cycad seed, use a medallion of cork or driftwood.

Materials

6 Kentucky coffee seeds

6 gingko seeds

1 cycad seed with the outer skin and flesh scraped off

6 head pins

1 metal bail

1 jump ring, 6mm in size

Tigertail, 1 yard (.9 m)

2 crimp beads

14 round gold beads, 6mm in diameter

Brown leather cord, 40 inches (101.5 cm)

4 ribbon crimps

Craft glue

Brown waxed linen thread, 4 yards (3.6 m)

5 jump rings, 4mm in size

1 clasp

Epoxy glue

Clear gloss enamel

Tools

Craft drill with a ⅟₁₆-inch (.16) drill bit and a set of small numbered drill bits

Felt-tip pen with water soluble ink

Wood-burning tool with pointed scribe

Wax paper

Toothpicks

Wire cutters

Small, fine metal file

Flat-nose pliers

Round-nose pliers

Crimping pliers

Scissors

Needle-nose pliers with serrated jaws

Large-eye sewing or embroidery needle to accommodate thread

Small paint brush

Instructions

One

Using the craft drill with the ⅟₁₆-inch (.16 cm) drill bit, drill holes lengthwise in the gingko and Kentucky coffee tree seeds.

Two

Use the felt-tip pen to draw spirals and straight lines on the surface of the cycad seed. With the wood-burning tool and pointed scribe, trace over the spirals by burning dots into the seed. For the straight-line figures, change the tip of the wood-burning tool to an angular or paddle-shaped tip. Burn the lines as shown. Wash the seed to remove any remaining ink.

Three

Drill a hole in the top of the seed with the craft drill and the ⅟₁₆-inch (.16 cm) drill bit. Attach the bail to this hole, squeezing the

bail tightly to secure it. Using the flat-nose pliers, attach the 6mm jump ring to the bail.

FOUR

Using the craft drill and a very small numbered drill bit, drill six holes in random spots on the shell of the cycad seed. Using a toothpick, mix a small amount of epoxy on the wax paper. Dip the end of each head pin into the epoxy and place the head pins into the holes in the cycad seed, pushing the head pins in as far as they will go. Allow the glue to harden.

FIVE

Use the wire cutters to trim the head pins flush to the surface of the seed. Using the fine file, file the head pins smooth to the surface of the seed, being careful to avoid scratching the seed.

SIX

String a crimp bead onto the tigertail. Using approximately ¼ inch (.5 cm) of the end of the tigertail, use the round-nose pliers to make a loop, then insert the end of the tigertail back into the crimp bread. Using the crimping pliers, crush the crimp bead to secure the end of the tigertail. Using the photograph as your guide, string the gingko seeds, Kentucky coffee tree seeds, and round gold beads onto the tigertail. When you've finished stringing the beads and seeds, string on a crimp bead, make a loop in the tigertail, and secure the end as you did above. Trim the end of the tigertail close to the crimp bead.

SEVEN

Determine how long you want the necklace to be. Depending on that length, cut eight pieces of leather cord accordingly. (For the necklace shown, each length was cut 5 inches (12.5 cm) long.) Apply craft glue to the inside surface of one of the ribbon crimps. Place the ends of four pieces of leather together side-by-side, and place them into the ribbon crimp. Using the needle-nose pliers, crush the crimp on the ends of the leather. Stretch out the leather and lay it flat. Trim the ends evenly. Using another ribbon crimp with glue in it, place the free ends of the four lengths into the crimp and crush the crimp using the needle-nose pliers. Repeat this process using the remaining four lengths of leather and the two remaining ribbon crimps. Allow the glue to dry thoroughly.

EIGHT

Cut eight pieces of waxed thread, each approximately 18 inches (45.5 cm) long. Using the needle and one piece of thread at a time, weave through the leather cord at four points along each length: close to each crimp; then two more times, spacing the weaving evenly down the length. Make sure to pull the thread tightly as you weave, so the cord ends will lie flat and close to each other. (See the photo below).

NINE

Using the flat-nose pliers and the 4mm jump rings, attach the leather sections to the beaded sections, and the clasp to the other ends of the leather sections. Using the remaining 4mm jump ring, attach the seed to the necklace at the midway point on the beaded tigertail.

TEN

Using the small paint brush, apply several coats of clear gloss enamel to the gingko seeds and cycad seed, allowing each coat to dry thouroughly before applying the next one.

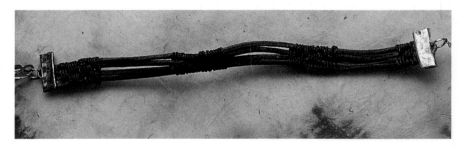

Packaging & Presentation

Making natural jewelry to give away is only half the fun. Use any leftovers from your projects such as twigs, leaves, grasses, pods, cones, even bones to make intriguing packages. If you're presenting a gift that will be opened immediately, you can use materials that are both fresh and fragile. Here are a few ideas to get you started.

Embellished Boxes are easy to make when you start with plain cardboard, wood, or woven-straw boxes from craft-supply stores. Have fun arranging cut or torn pieces of handmade paper and bits of natural materials, such as shells, beach glass, and raffia into simple and attractive designs.

When you have an arrangement that pleases you, glue the paper using white craft glue, then use a hot glue gun to attach the natural materials. You can also cover the top of the box with paper before attaching the natural materials, leaving the bottom of the container its natural color.

Leaf Packages are a way of using what's at hand since you begin by simply picking a few large and colorful leaves. If the season or location prohibits going outside for your wrappings, look to your house plants; they're often tropical in origin and have colorful and ample leaves. Croton (*Croton* spp.) leaves are some of my favorites because of their interesting and colorful patterns.

One-leaf packages are made by either folding a leaf over the jewelry or by rolling a leaf around it. To make them, start with a big floppy leaf and a few twigs or sticks. Trim each end of the twig and stick pieces diagonally to make sharp points. Then prewrap the jewelry in tissue paper or spanish moss to prevent it from poking holes in your wrapper.

For a fold-over package, lay the leaf on a flat surface, with its underside facing up. Place the prewrapped item in the middle of the leaf. Fold the sides into the center and hold them together with your free hand. Fold the stem end and the leaf point in toward the center, placing the stem end under the leaf point end. Secure all ends with the sharpened twigs or sticks, piercing the leaves through all layers as you would pin a piece of cloth with a straight pin. If desired, bind the package using raffia or string.

For a roll-up package, simply roll the prewrapped jewelry in the leaf and pin the end, as above, with a sharpened twig or stick, trimming the ends of the twig when finished. For a variation, use extra Spanish moss to create an attractive fringe.

Two-leaf packages are made with two matching leaves that are pinned together with sharpened twigs or sticks. Lay the item to be wrapped on top of one of the leaves, placing the other leaf on top. Make sure there is enough of a margin around the edges of the leaves, then pin. If desired, bind the package with raffia or string.

Leaf Packages, clockwise from bottom: banana leaf and pittosporum; caladium leaf and rose sticks; canna leaf and canna seed pods; croton leaf and Spanish moss; croton leaves with sticks and raffia; Center: loquat leaf with sticks.

Bamboo Containers make attractive gift packages or storage containers that are strong and lightweight. For the container shown you'll need: a length of bamboo that includes two nodes (the "joints" along its length); a fine-tooth saw or craft drill with a saw or cutoff blade; sandpaper or a sanding barrel for your craft drill; a 4-inch (10-cm) square of paper, leather, or fabric; string or cord (raffia, leather, hemp, etc.); scissors; craft glue; decorative paper; and small twigs.

Begin by using the saw to cut the bamboo crosswise to remove the top of the bamboo just under the top node. Then, use the saw to trim the bottom of the bamboo just under the bottom node. Sand any rough edges smooth. Note: The nodes provide a natural separating wall between bamboo sections. If you want a longer container, start with a longer length of bamboo and remove the wall inside between sections using a large drill bit.

Make the removable top of the container from the 4-inch (10 cm) square of paper, leather, or cloth by centering the material over the top of the bamboo and folding the sides down. Secure the top with string or cord, using a double knot. If desired, wrap the center of the bamboo with decorative paper; secure the paper with a string or cord, and slip in a decorative twig or piece of grass.

If you plan to re-use this container, use fabric for the cover and stiffen it so that it can take the wear and tear of frequent removals. To do this, mix equal small amounts of white craft glue and water. Saturate the fabric in

the glue and water mixture. Place a small square of wax paper around the top of the bamboo, securing it with a piece of string or a rubber band. Squeeze any excess glue and water from the fabric square. Place it over the wax paper, folding it around the top of the bamboo, and secure it with a string or rubber band. Leave the fabric top on the bamboo until it is dry and stiff; then remove it, discard the wax paper, and replace the top.

Drawstring Bags, quickly and easily stitched by hand, provide simple, soft packages for presentation and handy pouches for protecting pieces when they're not being worn.

For the bag shown you'll need: cardboard for your pattern; muslin or similar material; a pencil or fabric marker; scissors or rotary cutter; an iron; sewing thread and needle; embroidery thread or hemp string; a tapestry needle; and several beads (or seeds, twigs, etc.).

First, cut a rectangle from cardboard slightly larger than the finished size of the bag. Round two corners on one of the rectangle's short sides. Place this pattern on a double-thickness of fabric and trace around it with a pencil or fabric marker.

Cut out the fabric. On one of the short sides of each piece, fold over ⅛ inch (.3 cm) and press with the iron. Then fold again, making a ¼-inch (.5-cm) fold and press. Stitch the folded fabric on both pieces close to the folded edge. Do not sew the sides closed.

Place the two pieces with right sides together. Using a ¼-inch

(.5-cm) seam allowance all around, sew the two sides and bottoms together. On the sides, only stitch below the folded top edges. Turn the bag inside out and iron it smooth.

Cut two 12-inch (30.5-cm) pieces of embroidery thread or hemp string. Thread one piece on the tapestry needle and work it through one of the folded edges, then continue through the other side. Starting (and ending) at the other edge of the bag, work the other thread or string through both folded edges. String a few beads on the ends of the thread or string, knotting the ends to keep the beads in place. To close the bag, pull both pairs of thread ends on each side of the bag.

Sea Heart Boxes require time and patience to construct, since you're working with a fairly small object. An interesting choice you'll have to make is whether to leave the insides of the seed (the endosperm) in the finished box.

The endosperm of the sea heart is a hard, cream-colored substance stuck to the insides of the seed walls. t doesn't entirely fill the cavity, creating a small air pocket that enables the seed to float to distant shores.

To make the box shown, you'll need: one sea heart; ½-inch-wide (1.5-cm) masking tape; 3-inch (5-cm) square felt scrap; a vise; a fine-tooth saw or craft drill with a saw; craft knife; craft-drill attachments including small drill bits, a steel cutting burr (optional), and sanding and polishing wheels; small screwdriver; liquid furniture wax and paper towels (optional); sandpaper; rubber bands; craft glue; dollhouse (miniature) hinge with brads (nails); epoxy glue; small hammer or mallet; one head pin; one small seed and one small flat bead; flat-nose pliers; 4-inch (10-cm) length of 1mm black elastic cord; 1 crimp end for cord; wire cutters; one dangle pin; and round-nose pliers.

If desired, sand and polish the seed—this one was left with its natural matte finish. Since this seed is naturally thin, it requires precision in making a good, even cut, so you will need to carefully mark the cutting line. To do this, cut approximately 10 inches (25.5 cm) of the masking tape in half lengthwise, making two ¼-inch (.5-cm) strips. Place one strip of tape around the circumference of the sea heart, positioning one edge of the masking tape on your cutting line; this will be your guide when cutting the seed. Make sure the ends of the tape meet exactly and that the tape is smooth.

Cut the other strip of masking tape in half, making two 5-inch (12.5 cm) lengths. Place one vertically, centered on the flat surfaces of the seed, and the other horizontally, also centered on the flat surfaces of the seed. The vertical strip marks the positions for placing the clasp and hinge, while both strips will help you match up the halves of the seed once it's cut.

To cut the sea heart, first place it vertically in a vise. (The narrow rim with the masking tape will be "up.") To prevent the jaws of the vise from marring the seed, wrap it in a scrap of felt before placing it in the vise. Do not over-tighten or the seed may crack. With the fine-tooth saw, saw into the sea heart, using the edge of the masking tape as your guideline. Work an inch (2.5 cm) at a time, being careful to stay on the cutting line.

When you've sliced the seed in half, either keep or remove the endosperm. To keep it, scoop it out in the middle using a craft knife or a craft drill with a cutting burr. Don't cut too deeply, or you'll break through the endosperm. To remove it, pop each half out by using a small screwdriver as a wedge. If it doesn't pop out, use a screwdriver or craft knife to chip away at the endosperm. Once removed, use a paper towel to apply two coats of liquid furniture polish to the insides of the seed, polishing by hand or with a buffing wheel on a craft drill.

Remove the masking tape around the circumference of the sea heart. If the cut edges of the seed are rough, use sandpaper to sand them smooth. Then, using the vertical and horizontal tape strips as your guide, put the two halves back together, securing them with a rubber band.

To attach the hinge, position it on the seed, placing it evenly on either side of the cut. Temporarily glue the hinge to the seed with craft glue and allow it to dry. While the glue dries, determine which drill bit you'll use by testing different sizes on a scrap of wood. You want the brads to fit tightly to prevent the hinge from wobbling. When the glue is dry, drill through the holes in the hinge all the way through the seed's shell. Mix up a small amount of epoxy glue. Dip the hinge's brads in the glue and place them in the drilled holes. You may need to tap the brads in with the small hammer or mallet.

To make the clasp, decide which half will be the bottom. On that center front, drill a small hole using a drill bit that will accommodate the head pin you're using. (There is no standard size for head pins; different brands will require different size drill bits.) Thread a small bead or seed on the head pin, followed by a flat spacer bead. Insert the free end of the head pin through the hole in the seed. Using flat-nose pliers, make a tight bend in the head pin inside the seed. Trim the head pin with wire cutters, pressing the end close to the shell.

On the center front of the seed's top half, drill two holes large enough to accommodate the elastic cord, spacing them approximately ⅛ inch (.3 cm) apart. Thread the ends of a 3-inch (7.5-cm) length of elastic cord through each of the two holes to make a loop on the outside of the seed. Position the crimp end on the cord ends inside the seed, adjusting the size of the loop outside the seed so it is long enough to go over the seed on the head pin. Using flat-nose pliers, attach the crimp end, making sure the elastic is tight and secure. Use wire cutters to cut the cord ends and the crimp end, so that all edges are flush.

Trim the dangle pin to approximately 1 inch (2.5 cm). With round-nose pliers, make a loop approximately ¾ inch (2 cm) up from the bottom of the dangle. Place the dangle on the cord, then wrap the end of the dangle several times around the shaft to close the loop. Trim with wire cutters.

Tools and Materials Sources

Bones and Animal Materials

The Bone Room
1569 Solano Avenue
Berkeley, CA 94707
Phone: 510-526-5252
E-mail: evolve@boneroom.com
Web site: www.boneroom.com
Skulls, skeletons, insects, fossils, fossil casts, bone jewelry, animal remnants

Freeport Music, Inc.
41 Shore Drive
Huntington Bay, NY 11743-1322
Phone: 888-549-4108,
516-549-4108
Fax: 516-423-6550
E-mail: sales@freeportmusic.com
Web site:
www.freeportmusic.com
Horse hair (used, from bows of stringed instruments)

Jewelry Findings

The Bead Box
10135 East Via Linda, Suite C-116
Scottsdale, AZ 85258-5312
Phone: 602-451-4563
Fax: 602-451-1014
E-mail:
Beadbox@worldnet.att.net
Web site: www.beadbox.com
Beads, findings, chains, tools, books

Fire Mountain Gems
28195 Redwood Highway
Cave Junction, Oregon
97523-9304
Phone: 800-423-2319
Fax: 800-292-FIRE (800-292-3473)
E-mail: firemtn@cdsnet.net
Web site: www.firemtn.com
Beads, findings, chain, tools, books, bone beads, African porcupine quills, shark teeth

Garden of Beadin'
P. O. Box 1535
Redway, CA 95560
Phone: 707-923-9120
Orders: 800-232-3588
(800-Beadluv)
Fax: 707-923-9120
E-mail: beads@asis.com
Web site:
www.alserver.com/beadluv
Job's tears, rudraksha beads, porcupine quills, twig beads, seed beads (non-botanical), jewelry supplies & findings, books

Seeds and Plant Materials

AgroForester Tropical Seeds
P. O. Box 428
Holualoa, Hawaii 96725
Phone: 808-324-4427
Fax: 808-324-4129
E-mail: email@agroforester.com
Web site: www.agroforester.com
Bulk tropical seeds

The Banana Tree, Inc.
715 Northampton Street
Easton, PA 18042
Phone: 610-253-9589
Fax: 610-253-4864
E-mail: info@banana-tree.com
Web site: www.banana-tree.com
Exotic seeds in bulk

Brudy's Exotics
P.O. Box 820874
Houston, TX 77282-0874
Phone: 800-926-7333
Fax: 713-960-8887
E-mail: info@brudys-exotics.com
Web site: www.brudys-exotics.com

Bunch of Bloomers
3187 Keller Road
St. Thomas, PA 17252
Phone: 888-9-BLOOMER,
717-369-4951
E-mail:
bj@bunchofbloomers.com
Web site: www.bunchof-bloomers.com
Magnolia pods, lotus pods & seeds, cinnamon sticks, cloves, star anise

Burpee Gardens
W. Atlee Burpee & Co.
Warminster, PA 18974
Phone: 1-800-888-1447
Web site:
http://garden.burpee.com
Moonflower seeds

Chamberland Enterprises
6804 E. Highway 6 S., #315,
Suite 315
Houston, TX 77083
Phone: 281-933-2061
Fax: 281-933-1170
E-mail: chambec@chambec.com
Web site:
www.totalmarketing.com/chambec
Exotic plant seeds

Countryside Fragrances, Inc.
Countryside Herb Fram Brands
1420 Fifth Avenue-22nd Floor
Seattle, WA 98101-2378
Phone: 814-587-6331
Fax: 814-587-6047
E-mail: info@holidayscents.com
Web site:
www.holidayscents.com
Eucalyptus pods
(check availability)

Craft Supplies
Provo, Utah
Phone: 800-551-8876
Fax: 801-377-7742
E-mail: craftusa@craftusa.com
Web site: www.craftusa.com
Tagua nuts

Jungle Seeds Mail Order
Tropical Rainforest Seed Co.
P. O. Box 700
Hood River, Oregon 97031
Web site: www.tropicalrain.com

Legendary Ethnobotanical Resources
16245 SW 304th Street
Homestead, FL 33033
Phone: 305-242-0877
Fax: 305-242-9789
E-mail: info@ethnobotany.com
Web site: www.ethnobotany.com
Mescal beans, cinnamon seeds,
coffee beans, rudraksha seeds,
railroad vine seeds

Richter's Seeds
Goodwood, Ontario
Canada L0C 1A0
Phone: 905-640-6677
Fax: 905-640-6641
E-mail: orderdesk@richters.com
Web site: www.richters.com

SBE's Exotic Plant Seed Catalog
SBE
Seed Division
3421 Bream Street
Gautier, MS 39553
Phone: 1-800-336-2064
(order desk)
Fax: 228-497-6544
E-mail: seedman@seedman.com
Web site: www.seedman.com

Schusters of Texas, Inc.
Phone: 800-351-1493
Fax: 915-648-3194
E-mail: schuster@centrex.net
Web site: www.schustersoft-exas.com
Palmetto fronds, raffia, lotus
pods & seeds, twigs, palm fiber,
spanish moss, various pods

Sea Heart Company
P.O. Box 811, Station NDG
Montreal, Quebec, CANADA
H4A 3S2
Phone (orders): 888-732-4278

Phone: 514-489-6385
Fax: 514-489-7419
Website: www.seaheart.com
Wonderful sea heart gifts

Sea Shell City
708 Ocean Highway (1st Floor)
Fenwick Island, Delaware 19944
Phone: 302-539-9366
Phone: 888-743-5524
Fax: 302-539-1285
E-mail: seashell@dca.net
Web site: www.seashellcity.com
Sea beans

Tropical Treasures by Ellie Daniels
Phone: 1-888-SHELLS-2
(1-888-743-5572)
Fax: 1-941-566-9551
E-mail: shells@shells4u.com
Web site:
home.sprynet.com/sprynet/shells4u/shells.htm
Sea hearts, Sea beans, shark teeth

Tools

Alpha Supply, Inc.
1225 Hollis Street, Box 2133
Bremerton, WA 98310
Phone: 800-ALPHA 11
Fax: 800-ALPHA 44
Jewelry making tools and supplies

B & J Rock Shop
Dept J
14744 Manchester Road
Baldwin, MO 63011
Phone: 314-394-4567
Fax: 314-394-7109
Beads, findings, books

Bourget Bros.
1636 11th Street
Santa Monica, CA 90404
Phone: 800-828-3024,
310-450-6556
Fax: 310-450-2201
E-mail: borjay@worldnet.att.net
Web site: www.bourgetbros.com

Complete line of jewelry making
tools & supplies

Carolina Biological Supply Company
2700 York Road
Burlington, NC 27215
Phone: 1-800-334-5551 (sales),
Fax: 1-800-222-7112 (sales)
E-mail: carolina@carolina.com
Web site: www.carosci.com
Scientific apparatus, vasculums,
plant presses

Dremel
P. O. Box 1468
Racine, WI 53401
Phone: 800-437-3635
Web site: www.dremel.com
Motorized craft tools & accessories

Euro Tool
11449 Randall Drive
Lenexa, KS 66215
Phone: 913-338-3131
Fax: 913-338-3144
E-mail: info@eurotool.com
Web site: www.eurotool.com
Tools and supplies for jewelry
making

Lortone, inc.
2856 NW Market Street
Seattle, WA 98107-4279
Phone: 206-789-3100
Fax: 206-789-3102
E-mail: equipment@lortone.com
Web site: www.lortone.com
Rock tumblers

Wood

Black Jungle Terrarium Supply
P. O. Box 93895
Las Vegas, Nevada 89193
Phone: 800-268-1813,
702-795-4556
E-mail: info@blackjungle.com
Web site: www.blackjungle.com
Bamboo, palm wood, cactus
wood, cork bark, pumice

Further Reading

Beads and Jewelry

Doney, Mary. Jewelry. Danbury: Franklin Watts, 1996.
(An excellent beginners book with a multicultural approach to jewelry making.)

Dubin, Lois Sherr. The History of Beads. New York: Harry N. Abrams, Inc., 1987.
(An extensive, authoritative treatment of beads from all over the world.)

Francis, Peter, Jr. Beads of the World. Atglen: Schiffer Publishing, Ltd., 1994.
(THE BOOK on beads.)

Mack, John, ed. Ethnic Jewelry. New York: Harry N. Abrams, Inc., 1988.

Hunting and Gathering

Durrell, Gerald with Lee Durrell. The Amateur Naturalist. New York: Knopf, 1982.
(A great introduction to the natural world that includes excellent collecting methods.)

Kaplan, Eugene H. Southeastern and Caribbean Seashores; A Peterson Field Guide. Boston: Houghton Mifflin Company, 1988.

McConnaughey, Bayard H. and Evelyn McConnaughey. Pacific Coast. New York: Alfred A. Knopf, 1985.

Jewelry Making Techniques

Conner, Wendy Simpson. The Best Little Beading Book. La Mesa, California: Interstellar Trading & Publishing Company, 1995. (This is an excellent book for basic techniques.)

Glegg, Helen and Mary Larom. Making Wire Jewelry. Asheville: Lark Books, 1997.

LaFerla, Jane. Make Your Own Great Earrings. Asheville: Lark Books, 1998.

Simple Handmade Jewelry. Great Britain: Search Press Limited, 1993.
(Excellent projects from natural materials.)

Tomalin, Stefany. Beads! Make Your Own Unique Jewelry. New York: Sterling Publishing Co., Inc., 1988.

Seeds and Plants

Attenborough, David. The Private Life of Plants. London: BBC Books, 1995.
(This book is wonderful reading with lots of interesting facts.)

Balick, Michael J. and Paul Alan Cox. Plants, People, and Culture: The Science of Ethnobotany. New York: Scientific American Library, 1996.

Capon, Brian. Botany for Gardeners. Portland: Timber Press, 1990. (This is an excellent guide for the amateur gardener.)

Efraimsson, Raiff. 65 House Plants from Seeds, Pits, and Kernels. Santa Barbara: Woodbridge Press Publishing Company, 1977.
(A great introduction to gardening from your kitchen.)

Gunn, Charles R., Jr. and John V. Dennis. World Guide to Tropical Drift Seeds. New York: The New York Times Book Co., 1976.
(The book on world drift seeds. Unfortunately, this book is currently out of print. Consult your local library.)

Hargreaves, Dorothy and Bob Hargreaves. Tropical Trees Found in the Caribbean, South America, Central America, Florida, and Mexico. Lahaina: Ross-Hargreaves, 1965.

Pappas, Lou Sebert and Jane Horn. The New Harvest: A Cook's Guide to Exotic Fruits and Unusual Vegetables. San Ramon: 101 Productions, 1986.

Petrides, George A. Eastern Trees; A Peterson Field Guide. Boston: Houghton Mifflin Company, 1988.

Petrides, George A. and Oliva Petrides. Western Trees; A Peterson Field Guide. Boston: Houghton Mifflin Company, 1992.

Young, James A. and Cheryl G. Young. Seeds of Woody Plants in North America. Portland: Dioscorides Press, 1992.
(An excellent, scholarly book about seeds.)

Periodicals

American Craft
American Craft Council
72 Spring Street
New York, NY 10012-4019
Phone: 212-274-0630
Fax: 212-274-0650

The Drifting Seed, Charles R. Gunn, Jr., and Cathie Katz, editors. This is the newsletter of a growing group of people specifically interested in learning about and collecting drift seeds. For a copy contact Cathie Katz (Atlantic Press, P. O. Box 510366, Melbourne Beach Fl 32951).

Economic Botany
Scientific Publications Office
The New York Botanical Garden
Bronx, NY 10458

HerbalGram
The Journal of the American Botanical
Council and the Herb Research Foundation
P. O. Box 201660
Austin, TX 78720
Phone: 512-331-8868
Fax: 512-331-1924
(I read my first article on botanical jewelry in this periodical.)

Jewelry Crafts Magazine
4880 Market Street
Ventura, CA 93003
Phone: 805-644-3824

Lapidary Journal
Devon Office Center
60 Chestnut Avenue, Suite 201
Devon, PA 19333-1312

Ornament
P.O. Box 2349
San Marcos, CA 92079-2349

Pacific Horticulture
Pacific Horticultural Foundation
P. O. Box 22609
San Francisco, CA 94122

CONTRIBUTING ARTISTS

Richard Buckman, of Montreal, Canada, is an artist, writer, and entrepreneur. He shares his love for nature by empowering the sea heart to be his global peace ambassador.

George Corona is a Native American living in Arizona. His late wife taught him and his family to make dyed corn jewelry and to continue her love for the natural materials of their culture.

Judy Mallow is an artist in pine needle basketry and author of *Pine Needle Basketry*, published by Lark Books in 1997. She enjoys working with a variety of natural materials and lives in Eastern North Carolina.

Sharon O'Connell is a self-taught artist who creates jewelry in her "Tangled Web Studio" at the edge of a creek in Silverado, California. She specializes in pieces made from natural materials and from her own lampwork beads made from recycled glass.

Dyan Mai Peterson, is a nationally known gourd artist and teacher. She enjoys experimenting with any size or shape of gourd (which she mostly grows herself) to produce beautiful decorative bowls, jewelry, and dolls. She lives in the mountains of Western North Carolina.

Ruth Smith has been collecting and studying botanical jewelry for many years. She teaches classes on edible wild plants and lives in her colonial-era log cabin farmhouse in Virginia.

Robert I. Spragg Sr. is a self-taught artist who learned the old art of carving and turning tagua nuts. He lives in Davenport, Iowa.

Acknowledgments

I would like to thank the following people
for their encouragement, generosity, and
kindness in helping me with this book:

Cathleen Dunne

Ann Eason

Angelina Esparza

Mary Hilliard

Cathie Katz

Megan Keefe

Mike Luebe

Beverley Wilson

&

my editor, Jane LaFerla.

Index